THE HUNGRY SOUL

7 Steps To Ending Binge Eating, Emotional Eating & Food Obsession

ISBN: 978-1-91602-150-1 (paperback)
ISBN: 978-1-91602-151-8 (eBook)

CONTENTS

Introduction 1

My Story. Your Story. Our Story 9

The Hungry Soul 18

STEP ONE: AWAKEN TO THE DARK TRUTH OF
WEIGHT OBSESSION 23

A Nation Of Weight Watchers 24

Dieting + Feminism 27

Fixing The Broken Bits 32

Health At Every Size 35

B.M.I - Bullsh*t, Misleading And Inaccurate 43

Fat Shaming, Fat Phobia + The Fear Of Weight Gain 46

Diet Cult-ure 50

Why Weight Loss Won't Fix Your Problems 53

What I Now Know About Weight 56

What Are Diets? 59

When Healthy Eating Turns Harmful 65

The Minnesota Starvation Experiment......70

The Exploitation And Profit
Of The Diet Industry......72

Diet Statistics......81

Why Diets Do Not Work......89

STEP TWO: BODY NEUTRALITY IN A WORLD OF BODY PERFECTION......101

The Media + Body Image......102

Media Exposure + Body Image Ideals......106

Body Diversity And Social Comparison......115

Redefining Beauty......120

Body Neutrality - Not Body Love......124

STEP THREE: FEELINGS NEED TO BE FELT, NOT FED......131

Emotional Eating + Binging......132

You Can't Fight Physiology......138

Feel The Feels......141

Emotions Are Stuck In Food......151

STEP FOUR: DITCH THE DIETS......155

Take Your Power Back......156

The Perfect Way To Eat......159

Reconnect To Body Wisdom......165

Removing All The Labels 170

Switching Off Diet Mentality 175

Throwing Away The Scales 181

Satisfaction + Enjoyment 185

Leaving Scarcity Mindset Behind 191

Through The Lens Of Curious 194

Your Self Trust Muscle 196

Stop Waiting On Your Weight 198

STEP FIVE: OVERCOME YOUR SELF LIMITING BELIEFS **203**

Food For Thought 204

Your Undigested Story 210

Your Fearful Inner Critic 213

STEP SIX: FEEDING YOUR HUNGRY SOUL **217**

What Are You Really
Hungry For? 218

The Symbolic Substitute 222

Radical Truth Telling 226

Good Girls + Shy Rebels 230

Less Doing And More Being 234

STEP SEVEN: LIVING A FULL UP LIFE THROUGH SOUL NOURISHMENT **237**

Vitamin P Deficiency 238

Turning On The Woo-Woo 240

Find Your Sisterhood 244

Permission Is Everything 247

CONCLUSION - YOUR INVITATION **251**

BIBLIOGRAPHY **256**

RESOURCES **260**

ABOUT THE AUTHOR **261**

DEDICATION

To all women who are fighting food and their bodies.

To all women who believe losing weight will make them happy.

To all women who have bought into diet culture and lost precious time chasing slimness.

To all women who have beaten themselves up for binging, overeating or turning to food for comfort.

Finally to all women who have never felt good enough until the number on the scale tells them they are.

This is for all of you. It's time to take your power back.

INTRODUCTION

Imagine a life where there is no more guilt around food. No more disgust. No more telling yourself that was the last time you'll eat an entire packet of chocolate biscuits.

If you are anything like how I used to be, this seems like the ultimate fantasy. The elusive place you can only ever dream of getting to as heaven knows you've been trying for years now. Every time you try, you are convinced you'll finally solve your eating issues and body insecurities. Yet with each attempt of being good comes along more feelings of failure as you hear that inner critic telling you how weak willed you are and need to try harder.

Now I don't believe in coincidence, everything is synchronicity and you are here for a reason. Somehow in this crazy big world our paths have crossed and you've got this book. You and I were supposed to meet.

Maybe you know you want to break free from emotional eating or binging but you aren't sure how. Maybe you are wanting to become a 'normal' eater but have no idea where to start or perhaps you are fed up of feeling like you are fighting food and yourself all the time and just want to stop.

I get it. I get you.

That's where I used to be too not that long ago.

1

Since overcoming food obsession, binge eating and emotional eating, this is what I now know to be true; every woman has a right to feel amazing in her body, confident in her skin and enjoy everything she chooses to eat without guilt, disgust or shame. With the right guidance, I believe that any woman can reach that point and that includes you. You too can have that freedom, experience guilt free eating and feel body confidence like never before. You too can stop emotional eating, binge eating, food obsession or feeling like a crazy woman as soon as there is chocolate in the house. You too can stop panicking, stressing and getting anxious around food and stop devoting all of your time to calories, tracking, monitoring, measuring and judging yourself for all of it.

Whatever your reason for getting this book, you'll find the answers you are looking for.

Now I'm a pretty intuitive person and I am almost certain that I know more about you than you realise. So based on the fact you are here, is this you?

Do you find yourself thinking about food often throughout your day?
Are you either being 'good' on a diet, or falling off the wagon and inhaling everything in sight?
Do you eat or binge in secret hoping no one will see you or find out?
Do you feel guilty and ashamed with your behaviour around food?
Do you ever get frustrated and annoyed as to why you can't get a grip on this, after all you are a smart and intelligent woman and have succeeded in many areas of your life, just not this one?
Do you spend more time thinking, planning or worrying about food and eating than you do actually enjoying your life?
Does your food obsession control you and what you do?

If you answered yes to any of them, then you are in the right place gorgeous lady!

I know you are sick and tired of going around on this hamster wheel aren't you? Maybe you've been on it for years or what seems like a lifetime and you have had enough, questioning your sanity one too many times, especially when you've been unable to stop taking the chocolate biscuits out of the packet after you promised yourself 'I'm only going to have one!'

So how would you love a life where food was not your greatest concern or obsession? Where you no longer tried really hard to be 'good' only to start over again every Monday. Where your days no longer felt chaotic when it came to eating. I want to show you that by taking a different approach to this, anything is possible where binge eating, emotional eating and food obsession no longer stop you from living a life which fills you up.

I feel I need to mention that this book is a little unorthodox and will take you out of your comfort zone in many way but that is a good thing, nothing changes until we challenge ourselves. It is also categorically not to help you lose weight. Diets don't work as you will discover further on and besides I've tested them all to know that's true. It has, however, been written to help you gain clarity on why you fight food and your body and then give you the steps to start taking your power back as your relationship with food and with your body has got nothing to do with lack of willpower, lack of discipline, not trying hard enough or indeed not being good enough. It has though got everything to do with the way that you perceive food, the beliefs that you have around body image, your unsatisfied non-physical hungers and all of the BS stories which you have been brainwashed into believing for years by the weight loss industry, many of which I will be exposing here.

This book is to help you find your calmness, your balance and your peace. It's to help you gain a scientific and holistic understanding as to why, up until now, you've always thought it's been your fault; that you haven't had enough willpower to resist the chocolate, not enough discipline to stick to being 'good' or not tried hard enough, often beating yourself up about it for days. For all those times you felt like you were going crazy with your head in the fridge, I want to help you explore the reasons behind it as so much time, energy and life goes into maintaining this constant struggle with food.

IT'S TIME TO TAKE YOUR POWER BACK GORGEOUS AND RECLAIM YOUR LIFE!

I've personally experienced the dark side of this subject after having struggled with dysfunctional eating and weight obsession for 14 years, something which I believe is important that you know. Incase we haven't yet met, let me introduce myself.

I'm Rachel Foy, creator of The Food Freedom Masterclass and founder of Soul Fed Woman and I know how much food dominates your life.

Back in 2005, I had reached the peak of my own dysfunctional relationship with food and my body. I remember sat on the floor of my apartment, having inhaled an entire box of chocolate breakfast cereal, crying my eyes out, just wishing it would all stop. The obsession, the calorie counting, the guilt, the fear, the panic, the anxiety, the dieting. All of it. I wanted a way out of this destructive cycle which had eaten 14 years of my life at that point.

Fast forward some years later and I finally got what I wanted; I found my food freedom. I stopped binging and calorie counting, my body hatred disappeared and I found peace with who I was (cellulite, stretch marks and wobbly bits included.) Today I no longer obsess or count calories. I can't remember the last time I binged, I have no idea what I weigh even during and after my two pregnancies and I sometimes have cake for breakfast without ever feeling guilty for anything I choose to eat. Not anymore.

I've spent the last 10+ years of my life working with women like you, helping them understand that their relationship with food and their bodies is far more symbolic and metaphorical than they realise and I've trained and studied with some of the leading experts in their fields in order to facilitate the greatest level of transformation and freedom possible for everyone I work with. I'm an eating psychology mentor, a clinical hypnotherapist, a female empowerment coach, an anti-diet teacher and I'm also a mum to two small children, one of which is a daughter. I'll talk more about this later as it's very relevant to what we are discussing.

I'm going to share with you how you can use my experience, both personal and professional to learn and understand how to heal your struggle with food and your body, feed your own hungry soul and find yourself again, your true self and not the slimmer one you think you need to be in order to be happy.

Now in order to get the most out of this book, I'm inviting you to do several things.

Firstly be really open to the information I'm sharing. I realise that at this point you have probably wasted lots of money on books, guides and programs in the quest to find the perfect way to eat so you can have the perfect body but I am asking you from my heart to put aside everything that you think you know about food, eating and losing weight.

Secondly I am taking a random yet intuitive guess that you are incredibly good at being a bitch to yourself. Criticising yourself. Judging yourself. Telling yourself that you need to try harder. Am I right? I know I am as that's exactly what dysfunctional eaters end up doing when it comes to their food struggles and body image issues and honestly, it's not serving you, so it's time to let it go. Instead I invite you to explore everything through the lens of curiosity which involves turning down the critical and judgemental voice in your head. We all have to start somewhere and curiosity is a wonderful place to start. There is no room for criticism or judgement when you are working towards finding your food freedom. You have already spent far too long judging and criticising yourself so as of now, as you are reading this, I invite you to make a deliberate, intentional and conscious decision to stop the self criticism. Become really intrigued about who you are and what you do, how you react, how you respond to things and how you feel. I'll be guiding you throughout the book on how to practice this.

Thirdly I ask that you start to open up communication between yourself and your body. I know that sounds a little weird but let me explain. You are here as you struggle from some kind of food issue whether it be emotional eating, binge eating, overeating, stress eating or maybe you are a very restrictive and selective eater. Regardless of what your struggles are, the lack of communication that you have between yourself and your body is a huge piece of this jigsaw puzzle.

So many of us who constantly fight food spend our entire life living in our heads and in our thoughts. We think about how we should eat, we think about what we want to eat and we think about food all the time. What I would like to invite you to do instead is to start listening to your body more and more. Your body has so much intuitive wisdom when it comes to food and eating yet the more food obsessed you have become (and more than likely obsessed about your weight too so therefore dieted), the more you have inadvertently tuned out of this natural body wisdom. Re-connecting to your body wisdom begins by opening up communication to your body and I will be talking about your body using 'her' and 'she'......she isn't an 'it'. You'll also discover that your soul overlaps this body wisdom and when you are learning how to feed your hungry soul, being connected to your body is vital to hear the whispers of your intuition.

Next I ask that you begin the baby steps of becoming honest with yourself and speaking your truth. Change can only happen when we embrace our truth. The true nature of what's going on within our lives gives us a gateway to access the real reasons we feel unhappy and why we often deflect that feeling by blaming our body instead and turning to food as a coping strategy and a symbolic substitute for other things. Grab yourself a journal and go through the prompts and questions I've sprinkled throughout the book.

PEOPLE DON'T NEED TO BE SAVED OR RESCUED. PEOPLE NEED KNOWLEDGE OF THEIR OWN POWER AND HOW TO ACCESS IT.

Finally I am not here to save you. I'm here to help you remember what you've forgotten. When you embrace the divine power within you and allow your hungry soul to guide you with food as well as with life itself, you begin to embody and awaken the energy and essence of your Soul Fed Woman. Your authentic, confident, powerful and real self. It's my mission to help you realise that you have a Soul Fed Woman within you who is waiting to be recognised, heard and acknowledged. You've been ignoring her for far too long.

This book has been written from my heart and brings together years of working in this field and coaching hundreds of women to stop fighting food and their bodies. You'll see snippets from former clients or women within our community throughout the book as they share their own journey with you, some names have been changed for confidentiality reasons.

So if you are ready to learn and practice trusting yourself with food and not feeling that any slight deviation is complete and utter failure as you nibbled on a french fry or a bar of chocolate and you truly want to leave the chaos behind, I'm so excited as to what you are about to discover. This is about to be one of the most rewarding, empowering and liberating things you have done for yourself.

I believe in you

Love Rachel xox

My Story. Your Story. Our Story

My body was physically shaking as I sat on the floor watching the snow fall outside the window on that cold wintery February afternoon of 2005 in Munich, Germany. I hadn't long been back from work and I had that all too familiar sensation of feeling out of control. I had been unsettled all afternoon and I knew what was going to happen.

In the blink of an eye, I had eaten my way through an entire family sized box of chocolate flavoured cereal drenched in 2 litres of full fat milk. I was on autopilot, again. Feeling completely detached and unable to stop, yet knowing full well what I was doing. I felt so disgusted and ashamed of myself when I scraped the bowl clean as I felt the warm tears streaming down my face. Slumped on the kitchen floor, leaning against the cupboards, my body was quivering from overwhelming emotions and reacting to the copious amounts of sugar I had consumed in one sitting. I couldn't do this anymore. I had spent 14 years up until this point fighting with food, my body and myself and I was exhausted. Yet it hadn't always been that way.

My story started when I was 13 and like most teenagers I felt uncomfortable in my own skin. I was shy. Introverted. Not very confident. It would be years later that I discovered I was a very intuitive, sensitive empath who picked up on everything going on around her and groups of people were uncomfortable for me before I knew how to deal with them.

Despite having a really happy childhood, when I reached high school, like for so many of us, I felt like I didn't fit in. The insecurity I felt within myself soon became the start of my dislike towards my physical appearance. I blamed my curly hair, my braces, my body for not being slim enough, for having cellulite and for being a late developer; the latter being something which I remember being teased about for years. Throw into the mix my need to please people and seek approval from all sources except myself and you have a recipe for a pretty rubbish time at high school. I was a studious and slightly geeky adolescent, always striving for perfection in everything I did. 98% exam results were a failure in my eyes and coming second in something wasn't good enough. It's no wonder my weight and food obsession in the coming years took a hold as ferociously as it did.

Looking back at that time throughout school, I was so fearful of rejection and not being liked that it stopped me from being authentically myself. I was seeking approval from too many other sources and spent years searching for something, not realising it was my own approval and acceptance I needed. Instead I connected the 'something' to weight loss, believing I would feel better, have more confidence, be happier and be more accepted when I was 10lbs lighter. As is sadly so common in female circles, I had friends who began talking about their dissatisfaction with their weight as we flicked through the teenage magazines in the playgrounds, comparing our bodies to the popstars and models smiling back at us. All of our mums were on diets so it seemed like a normal thing to do. So I did. No-one was to blame and I certainly don't blame anyone for what happened when I innocently stepped on the diet wagon but that's how it started, my slippy slope into a world I never intended to be in. I exercised. I counted calories, points and Syns. Yet nothing really changed. I was so hungry for acceptance. I was so hungry to feel like I fitted in, like I belonged. I was so hungry to just be me, yet somehow being me didn't feel OK, it didn't feel good enough. So for the next 14 years I tried to change who I was by manipulating my body and starving my soul in the process.

As the years passed, not only did I finish colleague and start university but I also became a chronic dieter. Food completely took over. Obsessive and compulsive thoughts around eating, calories and my body filled so much space in my brain, there was little room for anything else. I didn't trust myself or my intuition and I loathed my body and how she looked. Anxiety, worry and fear around food and my weight became a daily occurrence with periods of actual panic attacks at the most inconvenient times, like during university exams or whilst sitting on a bus on my way to lectures. Deep down I never quite felt good enough, no matter what I did or achieved so I kept trying harder. Yet in amongst it all, my relationship with food and my body became increasingly more dysfunctional with each diet wagon I fell off. I didn't know at the time that diets never work and I never failed them, they failed me. So for 14 years my life revolved around diets and weight. Tracking. Measuring. Monitoring. Calculating. Binge eating. Food obsession. Emotional eating. Self Punishment. Exercise addiction. Self hatred. Self criticism. Judgement. Lots of judgement. Lots and lots of judgement.

MY WHOLE LIFE OVER THAT 14 YEAR PERIOD WAS BUILT ON THE FACT I WAS A WORK IN PROGRESS.

My relationship to food was like a giant pendulum swinging between being really 'good' or inhaling everything I could find. I sometimes resorted to throwing food away and squirting it with washing up liquid so as not to go back, except I did. I remember eating out of the bin on more than one occasion. I don't know what upsets me the most when I think about that now, how much food really did dominate my life or how little self respect I had at the time.

This love/hate relationship with food and my body was so explosive. One minute I could be eating something really delicious and the next my inner critic would be yelling, 'why did you eat that, I thought you were trying to lose weight? Wow you eat a lot! What's wrong with you??' And when I felt so bad and guilty I would always, without fail, put myself back on a diet at the beginning of the next week as that's when diets start, all in the hope of feeling better about myself for losing some weight but the inevitable always happened. I would feel so deprived and unsatisfied with the low-fat, fat-free, carb-free, sugar free diets that within days my cravings would descend like a black fog gripping so tightly I couldn't escape it and then I would find myself swallowing an entire cake or box of cereal without even chewing it. I was fed up, stuck in a life which didn't fill me up and in a body I hated.

Surprisingly no one knew about any of this as I hid it so well. It was a secret for a long time which I now know is really common. Most dysfunctional eaters keep it all behind closed doors and you can't tell by looking at someone to what extent they may be fighting food and themselves. Although I was never medically diagnosed with an eating disorder, I now believe I was suffering from BDD (Body Dysmorphic Disorder), Binge Eating Disorder (BED) as well as periods of Avoidant/Restrictive Food Intake Disorder (ARFID) and for a while I suffered with Orthorexia, where I would only eat clean and healthy foods whilst working out at the gym sometimes multiple times a day. I also experienced social anxiety and panic attacks on and off for years too. You could say my mental health was not in a great place for a little while back then.

So back to the chocolate cereal incident with me sobbing on the kitchen floor. After spending 14 years battling binge eating and food obsession whilst chasing the illusive dream of slimness believing that would be the key to the happy life door, my journey into overcoming my food struggles was about to start as there's something I forgot to tell you. Four months earlier, my fiancé called off our relationship and wedding. We'd been together for 8 years and had survived college and different universities, travelling to see each other at the weekends. After our graduations we both moved to Munich where I had landed my dream job at The European Patent Office yet three years into our German adventure, my world fell apart over night when he said he didn't want to be with me anymore. He'd been seeing someone at work for months, unbeknown to me of course. He was in love with her and they were moving in together.

Time stood still and sped up all at the same time. I can imagine that's what being sucked into a black hole must feel like. The most surreal and bizarre feeling. Shock I guess and disbelief. Complete and utter disbelief at what I had been told. Within the time it took him to say one sentence, not only did my world as I knew it change completely but I instantly lost my identity and my future as I'd planned it. I had no idea who I was. I didn't know where I was going. I didn't know what the future would now look like. What would I tell people? And the wedding, what about the wedding?! I didn't know whether to cry, scream, panic, hide or run away. As it turns out I did all of those things in the preceding months following that life changing conversation on that cold October evening.

As the final months of that year passed and the new year arrived bringing with it the freezing temperatures of the Bavarian winter, it was all a bit of a blur. I moved to a new apartment closer to my friends. I tried to pick the pieces up and figure out who I was and what the hell I wanted, but I couldn't. I was so confused, so hurt at the depth of betrayal. During this time, as is so common with relationship breakdowns, food was no longer my obsession. I completely stopped thinking about food, eating or my weight. I was trying so desperately to focus on getting through each day and surviving which seemed far more important. The obsession which had always been there, controlling and ruling my every waking thought, action and behaviour was pushed to the back of my mind for the first time ever. I became the slimmest I'd ever been without doing anything. Actually that's not true, I became the skinniest I'd ever been. Work colleagues and friends expressed their concern at my dramatic weight loss. I was boney. I wasn't eating. In fact some days I'd be getting ready for bed and realise I literally hadn't eaten anything all day, that's the extent of my connection to life. Food simply fell off the radar the same way my clothes were falling off my now boney body.

I'd reached my goal.

I'm telling you this as I got to that place I'd been desperately wanting to for years.

Food obsession stopped. Food no longer controlled me. My weight was at an all time low without even trying or dieting and the scales displayed a number I had never seen in my life before, far less than my goal weight I had held in my mind for years. I remember buying new jeans as my old ones kept falling off my protruding hip bones and being shocked at the size I could squeeze my body into. I stared back at the figure in the dressing room mirror. I looked so skinny. Yet I couldn't feel anything.

I certainly wasn't happy.

It was so far from the 'happy life' I had imagined it would

be. I'd believed for years that slimness would make me giddy with joy and yet here I was finally slim wearing clothes two dress sizes smaller but instead of elation and feeling alive at my goal having been achieved, I was clawing frantically to pick the pieces of my life back up. It was so different to what I'd held in my mind for years, all the times I used that image as inspiration when I was pounding the treadmills in the gym. There was an emptiness which no number on the scale or label in my jeans could take away.

For months I drifted in and out of life, most of it I can't remember. I went out too much. I drank far too much. I held down my job with almost daily hangovers and very little sleep only to go back out each night and do it all again. I numbed myself from the reality I was in as I didn't know what else to do as I couldn't handle the truth. As the weeks turned into months and the first buds of the beautiful Bavarian spring appeared on the trees, I too started to emerge from my hibernation, taking baby steps to tentatively plug myself back into life once more. Yet as I started to allow life to flow through my veins, I was reacquainted with an old friend I thought I'd seen the back of. The fight with food started knocking on the door, uninvited. I found myself overeating, I was craving sugar on a daily basis and within what felt like a nanosecond I was back to my old dysfunctional relationship with food which had been missing for months at this point. Except this time was different. It was worse. Now I was terrified of eating. I was panicked at the thought I'd put all the weight back on and then I would have failed in the biggest way possible. I honestly didn't appreciate that my body had been under fed for months and she was literally in starvation mode and was making me eat whether I wanted to or not.

And so there I was, binging in the kitchen in my new apartment, feeling lonely and unhappy, drowning in a sea of guilt for having eaten so much whilst not knowing what to do with the waves of panic washing over me. I finally admitted to myself the severity of the situation and realised I needed more than my friends to support me through the break up. I accepted that my mental and emotional health was not in a good place and that's when my journey started. I sought professional help initially for stress induced health issues but it turned out to be for everything. I started prioritising myself and digging deeper into who I was more than I'd ever done before and the rest is history.

Nine months after my world had fallen apart, on a quick trip back to the UK to visit my sister, I was introduced to the best man for her up coming wedding. I didn't really believe in fate or divine intervention back then, now I totally do, the universe really does have your back. Simon was gorgeous. He was kind, caring, funny, handsome and all the things I could ever want in someone. I knew. We knew. It all happened so quickly yet it felt so right and within a year I'd left my job, re-located back to the UK, we'd moved in together, got engaged and started planning our wedding. We've been married for 11 years now, have a son and a daughter, we've lived in Dubai for a little while before settling back in the UK and I feel totally blessed and so grateful for how my story unravelled in the end.

I can honestly say that I have found my freedom with food and with myself as when I recall that version of me who was fighting it constantly, it's so upsetting and heartbreaking how much time I lost to that. Nowadays is a whole different story. I no longer count calories, measure or track what I'm eating. I don't weigh myself, I don't beat myself up when I eat too much of my favourite things and my time is now spent living rather than working out calories or monitoring what I've eaten that day. I have my life back.

I reflect on it all and truly believe that my 14 year battle was the greatest gift and blessing I was given so I can really understand and help other women like you break your own self destructive cycle of food dysfunction and body insecurities.

Your freedom is waiting for you.

Let me show you how to take it back.

THE HUNGRY SOUL

"To a hungry soul food is an obsession, to a satisfied soul food is just food"

When I first started working with women who were struggling with body insecurities, binge eating and emotional eating whilst spending hundreds, if not thousands of hours learning, understanding and mastering the craft of how our minds work, I started to realise something.

As women began reporting feeling more confident, they stopped binge eating.

As women started saying how less stressed they felt and how much more in control of their lives they felt, they weren't emotional eating anymore.

As women started saying how much more like themselves they felt, sometimes for the first time ever, their food and weight obsession disappeared!

As women started noticing how they felt enough, in the body they were in, no longer feeling the need to be anything more than they already were, their body insecurities became a thing of the past!

Witnessing this, first hand, was like a light bulb going off in my head. It all made sense. I realised that healing our relationship with food and our body is ultimately about healing our relationship with ourselves, becoming and awakening our own Soul Fed Woman now, not 10lbs from now, as it was never about the food. Food struggles were symbolic. They were metaphorical. They showed up when women were not Soul Fed. That is what happened to me and excitingly what was beginning to happen to my clients and other women within my community. The more soul fed they became, the more satisfied in their life they felt, the more connected to their true authentic self they were and the more they spoke their truth. The more they declared what they wanted and the more they stopped worrying about what others thought of them by doing more of what they wanted to do and stopped following the rules, the less their food struggles had any kind of control over them. This understanding lead me to appreciate just how many women suffer from Hungry Soul Syndrome and who are living their lives without ever feeding their soul what it's truly hungry for.

Food obsession, eating dysfunction and weight fixation are symptoms of someone with hungry soul syndrome and are ways of numbing out of reality for whatever reason. I've worked with women over the years who have turned to drink, smoking or compulsive shopping as a way of coping with life yet food and weight seem to be the biggest symptoms, especially amongst women.

I believed for 14 years that I wasn't good enough until I lost weight. I wasn't happy enough until I lost weight. I wasn't this enough or that enough. I wasted those years being a diet obsessed insecure individual who suffered from low self esteem, feelings of inadequacy and debilitating anxiety with panic attacks thrown in for good measure. I was hungry for so much more in my life, yet I didn't realise it at the time nor did I have any idea what I was hungry for.

I thought food was my problem. I thought the size, shape and weight of my body was the barrier keeping me from my happiness. I thought my lack of willpower was my issue.

I thought my inability to stick to plans, programs and regimes was the reason I felt like I did. None of that was true though for as it turned out I'd later discover that my struggles with food were symptomatic, symbolic and metaphorical.

I had a hungry soul which left me starving for much of my adolescence and my 20s and I didn't even know it! All I knew was that I wanted to lose weight in the belief I would feel better about myself and then life would improve.

Stuffing down an entire cake fed me momentarily but the hunger returned, always returned and so did guilt along with shame and then disgust. Without realising it food had become my biggest source of pleasure, happiness, comfort, contentment and satisfaction. It had become the replacement for the job I felt bored in, the relationship I felt insecure in and the country I felt disconnected to. Trying to fix the 'food & weight stuff' got me nowhere except down a path of food obsession and binge eating with even more body hatred and weight fixation whilst my happiness didn't improve. My self esteem didn't get better. Ultimately nothing changed. Even when I lost weight I still felt unhappy and not enough so I'd move the goal posts and see if I needed a new number to aim for.

So what is a hungry soul?

It is an insatiable appetite for something. A deep hunger. It's an emptiness, void and permanent hunger for more. A feeling that something is missing but you can't quite put your finger on it.

When our souls are hungry, they are starving for something. It could be adventure, travel, meaningful connections to people, joy, pleasure, passion, excitement, acceptance, authenticity and so many other things. All the things which we, as humans, have a right to experience and have in our lives. Yet sadly many of us don't, which leaves us feeling unsatisfied, empty and hungry for more. These non-physical hungers will never be found in the places you might be looking at the moment.

So how do you know if you have a hungry soul?

Well if you are reading this book as the title caught your attention and you know that you want to have a healthier relationship with food and your body, then you have a hungry soul gorgeous.

We turn to food for so many reasons other than physical hunger don't we? When we are stressed we reach for chocolate. When we've had a bad day we open the biscuits. When we are overwhelmed with life in that moment we distract ourselves with the contents of the kitchen cupboards, vending machine or supermarket aisle and temporarily we may feel better. However, the reality is that food, in that instant, is really a substitute for something else.

Chocolate becomes a substitute for relaxation and a moment to just breath in-between the monotonous yet busy day which has now become your life. Biscuits become a substitute for switching off from the overwhelm and the 1001 bubble gum thoughts in your mind which won't disappear, no matter how many times you write them down on your 'to do' lists or try and ignore them, whilst wine becomes a substitute for self care after you've been rushing around like a mad ass women all day and only had chance to sit down now and it's almost time to go to bed.

We end up feeding our feelings without truly recognising it.

Lucy: It was never about the food

....

When I completely lost all control around food, I always believed that I was somehow to blame. I blamed my lack of willpower, my lack of commitment, my lack of discipline and a multitude of other reasons. I never once stepped back from what I was doing to actually see it for what it truly was. It was symbolic. It was symptomatic. It wasn't about the food. It was never about the food.

So before we get into any more of this, let's start at the beginning of this journey by taking a look at your current relationship with food and your body and what role the diet industry and diet culture has been playing. Trust me, this topic cannot be ignored.

STEP ONE:
AWAKEN TO THE DARK
TRUTH OF WEIGHT
OBSESSION

A Nation Of Weight Watchers

I'm a truth teller so here's your first truth bomb. It's your desire to lose weight or maintain your weight which is driving the issues you have with food. I have never come across anyone who struggles with binge eating, over eating, food obsession or emotional eating who isn't either an active dieter, yo yo dieter or is weight conscious.

Even though it pains me to say this, straight off, I get it. We're women. We're *constantly* sold the idea that our bodies are not good enough, that we should be trying to improve our shape, tone up, lose weight, lose fat, lose inches and be on some kind of diet or another.

Media, magazines and advertisers sell us the idea that we should be relentlessly preventing the ageing process. We need creams for our wrinkles. Creams for our cellulite. Creams to make our boobs perkier and cream to lift our backsides and make them appear more voluminous! So it's no surprise that wanting to manipulate our bodies through food control is part of this conversation. Many of us spend years even decades of our lives chasing this vision we hold in our minds of having the perfect body, one which is flawless, blemish free and 'ideal' from society's point of view at least.

We use it for inspiration when we tell our partner we can't go for pizza tonight as we are 'trying to be good.' We use it for motivation when we are running on the treadmill for the 5th time this week, feeling light headed for pushing ourself too hard. We hold it in our mind when we jump on the scales in the morning after we've stripped ourselves naked and made sure we've completely emptied our bladder and we also blame our body for not being 'perfect' when we are squeezing ourselves into clothes which are clearly designed for the models who wear them in the magazines and not for a woman who has given birth twice.

This compulsion to measure and track brings us together in the funniest of ways. You might not have realised but one of the biggest and most socially accepted ways of being included and accepted into a group or community is through dieting. Diet groups gather in church halls, they hang out online together and they chat in facebook groups across the globe and that sense of belonging is something which holds us together. It's what human beings crave. We all seek acceptance and approval. Think about it, how many times have you partaken in diet talk over coffee or standing in the playground at school or on the phone to a friend? How many conversations have you overheard as a group of women criticise their bodies and themselves in front of each other, 'I put 2lb on this week and I don't know how, I thought I was being good.' I've had complete strangers at the checkouts in shops start talking to me and within minutes a reference has been made about weight gain and going on a diet as she unloads the contents of her basket in front of me, steely determination in her eyes as she looks at all the 'healthy' food on display. It's crazy but also understandable.

Our desire to be accepted and included in a group or community runs deep within us. Generations ago our survival depended on being accepted within our ancestral community. If we weren't liked and got thrown out, the likelihood of starvation or being killed by a wild animal was real, so we did whatever we could to fit in and be liked. We might not be fighting off wild animals whilst living in caves anymore but there is still a part of us even now, that really old lineage of generations before us which continues to run through our veins of needing to be accepted. Dieting truly is one way in which women are brought together, where complete strangers instantly have commonality, criticising their bodies and food choices and everyone supports them for doing so. If you've ever been a member of a slimming club, you'll know what I mean. Strangers sat around applauding the people who have been 'good' that week and offering encouraging words to the ones who have been 'bad.' It still brings people together.

It took me a long time to realise that we can still belong without everyone liking or accepting us. Feeling like we belong is an inside job as when you are at peace with who you are, it doesn't matter what the outside world thinks.

Anyway, I bet you're curious as to where this obsession, fixation, admiration and desire for losing weight even comes from aren't you?

DIETING + FEMINISM

The body shaming and diet talk which women are socialised into is part of patriarchy and is a distraction from us achieving equality - Rachel Foy

The standards to which women are held are more extreme and more unrealistic than ever before. Bodies nowadays communicate more about status than they ever have and are the reason for so much anxiety, stress and feelings of inadequacy. The pressure to be thin is around us all the time. Whether we want to be or not, we are exposed to advertising which is saturated with subliminal messaging that our self worth is determined by the size of our clothes and our over all appearance. Women are taught, and have been throughout history, to believe that it is totally ok to go to war with our bodies. Society tells us as women we should want to become slimmer so as to take up less space on the planet in the belief that will somehow make us better and more sought after individuals. We see it in magazines and in movies all the time, the hot skinny girl gets the guy and the larger curvier friend finds the dating scene more challenging. Might I point out it's always the girls, never the boys.

So many of us also believe that, as women, we are not allowed to have desires and it's wrong to say what we want. We think pleasure is frowned upon and we shouldn't want to take up space in the world so we follow the good girl handbook, do the right thing and stay in the shadows. Instead we obtain our pleasure and desires through eating and the notion of taking up space in the world manifests itself as fighting with the size of our bodies which socially is heavily influenced.

This perception of what women should be like goes back generations and despite things changing significantly from how our great great grandmother's lives were, we are still holding onto so much of this old way of thinking. For example, our female ancestors were far less independent than what we are nowadays and finding a mate, to essentially take care of them, was often connected to beauty and attraction. Your great great grandmother would not have had the freedom to do what you desire to do and create a life on her terms. Not back then. So emphasis was placed on appearance and taking 'care of oneself' so women wouldn't be left without a partner to financially look after them. In a 1950s Good Wife Guide it states…. "*don't forget to look as attractive and bright as possible for him*" Housewives were also encouraged to fight the temptations of the kitchen and keep an eye on their weight. As Jill Fisher advised in her lists of Do's and Don'ts for *The Irish Housewife* annual, "*Don't drink continuous cups of tea if you want to get your weight down. Don't eat potatoes for lunch just because you have cooked them for the kiddies.*"

Most of us have been on so many diets throughout our life that it has become a part of accepted behaviour. No one bats an eyelid when women are talking about dieting and losing weight as it's just what we do (you never overhear men talking about their bodies and weight the way women do.) Yet by encouraging or pressuring our friends and colleagues to partake in the conversations and the diets, we are also part of the problem as we're spreading and reinforcing the message that they too are not enough unless they slim down with us. We have all tied our worth to our weight as this obsession oppresses women by undermining their worth as anything more than a physical object and one which 'should' look a certain way.

Our society has such a preoccupation with 'perfecting' the female body that not only has dieting become accepted, it is also admired. From magazines to tv shows, conversations over coffee or standing in a school playground, you'll hear women across the globe say things such as "did you lose weight?? Wish I had your willpower" or 'what have you been doing? You look like you've lost weight.' In halls up and down the country women line up to receive their certificates for being the biggest loser of the week along with respect from their group and the admiration and external validation which they are so desperately seeking. All over the carefully curated feeds of instagram we see women working their butts off in the gym with the hashtag noexcuse whilst a lycra wearing mum shows off her six pack and carefully pre portioned food in the kitchen as she smiles into the camera with her 3 children hanging off her. As you look into her eyes all you can hear her say is 'so what is your excuse today??'

I came across a quote by Naomi Wolf that resonated so deeply with my own beliefs. In The Beauty Myth, Wolf writes, "A culture fixated on female thinness is not an obsession about female beauty, but an obsession about female obedience. Dieting is the most potent political sedative in women's history; a quietly mad population is a tractable one."

Convincing women that they are inadequate, not enough and must try harder effectively silences them from speaking up and becoming change makers within society.

It takes their power away.

It stops them standing in their truth of being powerful human beings just as they are.

It's impossible to speak up for what we believe when we are starving hungry all the time.

It's impossible to instigate change when our brains aren't working properly as we are trying to eat 1000 calories all day. It's impossible to stand in our truth when we feel so inadequate as our body isn't yet perfect and we believe we won't be accepted until it is.

Dieting and weight loss efforts imprison women.

Dieting is violence towards the female form.

Dieting encourages women to take up less space in the world and to become smaller and less.

I repeat, to become less of themselves!

Have you ever thought about it like that before?

Now I know that men are affected as well but, speaking from the view point of being a woman, having been a diet junkie myself and working predominantly with women, I truly believe that it is not to the same degree that women are affected. Almost all body insecurity products are aimed at women not men, think face creams, cosmetic surgery, underwear which smoothes your bumps, cellulite cream, hair dyes, false eyelashes, false nails....I could go on and on with this. The thought of men buying penis enhancement pads or pec enhancement pads sounds ridiculous, yet women can buy the equivalent in pretty much any department store and no one would say a thing.

This entire topic has become so normalised we can't even see that there is nothing normal about it. A few decades ago, if someone had an issue with their eating and their body, they would likely have gone and found help. A therapist. A counsellor. A psychologist. Yet nowadays food dysfunction and body shaming is so engrained as normal behaviour that we no longer talk about it as the significant social problem it has become. Feeling inadequate about our bodies, feeling scared of what to eat, scrutinising ourselves and checking our weight on a daily basis has become normal. Except it isn't. It is so far from normal it is really shocking to see what our culture has created.

No behaviour which could be seen as destructive and harmful with the potential of seriously affecting our quality of life and our mental health is ever considered 'normal.'

So why is this any different?

I'm not calling anyone anti-feminist for wanting to lose weight by the way as firstly weight control is addictive and secondly look at the society we live in. What I am saying though is there is a better way of nourishing yourself, one which isn't based on self hatred and feeling inadequate. After all, you can't take care of something you don't like.

DIETS TEACH US THAT FOOD IS THE ENEMY.
FOOD ISN'T THE ENEMY, SELF HATE IS

FIXING THE BROKEN BITS

You are perfectly imperfect just as you are and certainly don't need fixing. - Rachel Foy

You are reading this book as you want a solution to overcoming your food obsession, binge eating and over eating, so in order for me to show you how to do that, I have to tell you some home truths which you might struggle with initially. One of those truths is around weight loss.

I had a conversation with someone recently who asked me 'where is the harm in someone wanting to lose some weight...?'

Listen I'm not here to tell you what you have to do or indeed what you should do. That comes down to you deciding what is best for you at the end of the day. It's got nothing to do with me. However, at the core of wanting to lose weight and therefore diet, are many many things which we do need to talk about and recognise as individuals but also collectively as women.

One of them is the belief that we must be broken and need to be fixed as we view our bodies as not being 'enough' or not 'normal.'

How many times have you caught a glimpse of your naked body whilst getting out of the shower and thought 'I need to get rid of that wobbly tummy, it shouldn't look like that..?' I used to spend hours every day prodding my thighs in disgust, hating them, wishing they weren't as big and wobbly as they were. I felt like certain parts of my body made me inadequate in some way and that people would judge me based on them. This used to be my internal dialogue for over a decade and kept me trapped in the diet/binge cycle. Now don't get me wrong, I never viewed myself as being perfect in all other areas of my life, however, my distorted and dysfunctional relationship with food and my body was an area which I truly hand on heart believed was somehow broken. I searched for the solution to fix this for over a decade. Trying to fix it with diets. Trying to fix it with willpower, discipline and abstinence. Trying to fix it through extreme exercise. Trying to fix it by following eating plans, guidelines, rules and joining diet cults.

Yet all of my attempts to 'fix' my broken body never lead to anything other than more binges, lower self-esteem and an even more distorted view of myself, my body and my place within the world.

Unbeknown to me back then, I actually wasn't broken. I've never been broken and therefore I never needed to be fixed. I was a whole human being with perfect imperfections, none of which ever needed to be fixed. It took me many years to realise this.

And I'd like to highlight this for you now.

YOU ARE NOT BROKEN

Dieting and our desire to lose weight is fuelled by lack of self worth, lack of feeling good enough, lack of compassion, lack of kindness to self, lack of happiness and satisfaction in life and a lack of liking who we are.

Don't believe me?

Well does anyone diet to lose weight as they already fully like themselves?

Does anyone diet to lose weight as they are happy about who they are?

Does anyone diet to lose weight as they believe that they are already good enough?

Does anyone diet to lose weight as they believe they are already worthy enough?

Does anyone diet to lose weight as they are compassionate and kind towards themselves?

Does anyone diet to lose weight as they are already so happy, satisfied and fulfilled in their lives?

Does anyone diet to lose weight as they are already unconditionally accepting of who they are?

NO!

Those are all the reasons why people go on a diet as they think weight loss will bring about all those things which they want but it doesn't work that way. Until you feel good enough and worthy enough, until you like who you are, until you show yourself kindness, respect and self compassion, until you acknowledge who you are and what you've been through and until you feed your soul exactly what it is hungry for, you will find yourself on the weight loss journey indefinitely whilst battling and fighting food along the way because losing weight isn't the solution to any of those things.

They will all still be missing even if your waist line shrinks. What's more is we're not the ones who are broken, the system known as society is broken for that decides whose body is acceptable, worthy and valuable.

So if you could make the decision and the choice right now, to stop trying to fix yourself and your body, how would your life be different? It's a question worth pondering.

HEALTH AT EVERY SIZE

Wait......

What about needing to lose weight for health reasons?

You may be reading this thinking, 'well I get what she's saying but….. I am over weight and I do need to lose weight for my health otherwise I'll get diabetes or heart disease and my doctor has told me to lose weight too.'

OK. I hear you and I'm taking a deep breath for this argument comes up frequently.

Health is a multi dimensional and multi complex topic. When we, society, particularly the medical and health profession start saying that overweight people need to lose weight to be healthy, what we are really saying is that health is only about the size of someone's body based on physical appearance. It's solely about the size of their legs, arms, tummies and body parts.

Surely health is about many factors, isn't it? What about our emotional health? Psychological health? Spiritual health? What about our habits, behaviours and patterns? What about how happy we are at the moment and how satisfied with life we feel?

Our weight is one tiny factor in a much greater picture.

DOCTORS BUY INTO THIS DEEPLY HELD CULTURAL ASSUMPTION AROUND WEIGHT THAT FAT IS BAD AND THIN IS GOOD EVEN

MORE SO THAN THE REST OF US

If someone visits their doctor with an illness you'd assume they'd receive empathy and support, yet if they have a larger body they are frequently met with eye rolls and skeptical questions let alone having treatment delayed or even denied. Doctors are supposed to be a patient's ally to healing yet for fat people, they are frequently the source of judgement, upset and blame. It doesn't matter what condition or issue the patient presents with, it doesn't matter how much pain or discomfort they are in as the first thing they often hear is that it would improve if they stopped eating so much. Surely healthcare assessment should be based primarily on symptoms and behaviour rather than weight? We can't make assumptions about someone's health purely looking at their body. Morally and professionally that isn't acceptable. I've had plenty of clients over the last 10 years report this from their own personal experience and weight discrimination can also go the other way too. I've heard of patients being denied access for eating disorder treatment because based on their weight and BMI they weren't 'sick or thin' enough to be accepted. Whatever way it presents itself, weight discrimination is real and it shouldn't be.

ESME: APPARENTLY FAT PEOPLE CAN'T HAVE EATING DISORDERS

....

A few years ago I lost quite a significant amount of weight although it wasn't the first time I'd done that. I'd get up and the first thing I'd do was smoke some cigarettes to suppress my appetite, I lived on yoghurt and fruit throughout the day and tried to replace solids with liquids in whatever form I could. My head would be spinning with dizziness at work as I was so hungry but the longer I carried on, the more I didn't want to stop. I'd collapse on my sofa when I came home, sometimes falling asleep for hours as I was constantly exhausted. A close friend of mine started questioning if I was OK as she'd noticed my erratic behaviour and she knew something wasn't right as did I. It was a huge step for me to go and see my doctor as I had known for months that my food obsession and desire to lose even more weight had now become an issue. I was feeling anxious whenever I was eating, my periods had become irregular and my mood swings were horrific.

I told my doctor I'd lost several stone in the last few months by eating very little even though I was wearing UK size 18. You know what he said? He looked me up and down and said that whatever I'd been doing was working and to look at adding a few more hundred calories to my daily intake as once I was smaller, I wouldn't need as much food anyway.

If you looked at everything I'd said, other than my weight and the size of my body, it was clear to see I was in the early stages of having developed an eating disorder and here he was congratulating me.

Public health still talks about obesity as a lifestyle or ignorance issue, an information deficit - people who don't know about calories accidentally eating too many of them. This simply isn't true and it's an ignorant assumption to make nor is it helpful. Someone's body size is not, in isolation, indicative of their overall health or happiness nor should it be. We have to start changing the conversations around weight and health, firstly with ourselves and then with friends, family and doctors.

The reality is that more than 97% of dieters regain everything they lose and more within 3 years yet many weight loss studies for obesity and health research rarely follow individuals for more than 18 months making their results questionable and potentially down right deceptive. In research I came across, studies from the Centre for Disease Control and Prevention repeatedly found the lowest mortality rates among individuals whose BMI was overweight or mildly obese. What's more in research from UCLA and the University of Minnesota, it is suggested that losing weight for health reasons doesn't actually improve health biomarkers; "changes in diastolic and systolic blood pressure, fasting blood glucose, cholesterol and triglyceride levels were small, and none of these correlated with weight change." In their summary they stated, "in correlational analyses, we uncovered no clear relationship between weight loss and health outcomes related to hypertension, diabetes, or cholesterol, calling into question whether weight change per se had any causal role in the few effects of the diets. Increased exercise, healthier eating, engagement with the health care system, and social support may have played a role instead."

So basically weight loss is not directly related to improving health. Now that's interesting.

In 2013 the American Medical Association (AMA) re-defined obesity as a disease, meaning from that point it could be treated as such with medical intervention, although it clearly isn't a disease and it is not always harmful but the medical profession by enlarge is biased towards fat people, reinforcing this fat phobic society in which we live. Not only that but there's a lot of money at stake in treating obesity with insurance companies often covering treatment expenses, something they couldn't do prior to 2013.

I cannot think of any other disease, remembering that obesity is labeled as such, where treatment rarely works and people are blamed for not recovering. That's not right is it?

In fact dieting and weight cycling or yo yo dieting leads to unhealthy physical and psychological effects within the body. In fact yo-yo dieting, which is incredibly common amongst dysfunctional eaters, has actually been shown to be linked to potential health issues such as heart disease, higher blood pressure, inflammation and insulin resistance and, ironically, long-term weight gain as well as food dysfunction! So, in effect, it creates the very health issues which we are being told we can avoid by losing weight?! Yes that's pretty much it.

If you have struggled with food in any sense, you'll know first hand how rigid, restrictive and fearful eating will cause psychological issues such as anxiety, insomnia, heart palpitations and maybe even panic attacks. Is that healthy? What long term effects could that have on your body? Do not underestimate the detrimental implications which weight and food obsession has on our health, especially our emotional health which in turn, does affect our physical health. Now bearing that in mind, do you think that someone who no longer obsesses about their body, no longer binges, no longer turns to food for emotional support or comfort and no longer uses food as a way to fill any emotional voids would be healthier than someone who is struggling with all of those things?

Absolutely. And even if they were in a larger body, they would still be healthier overall.

At the peak of my weight and food struggles, I was not healthy. I lived in a constant state of anxiety and fear. I didn't sleep well. I self medicated with food and wine using both as a drug and I had heart palpitations due to the stress I placed on my body through rigorous exercise combined with restrictive eating. The crazy part is that I had a socially acceptable body size and a 'normal' BMI but I was not healthy and I dread to think what could have happened to my health in the long term if I had carried on doing what I was doing to myself.

So if you believe your weight needs to come down for you to

be healthier I want to encourage you to begin focusing your attention away from your weight, your body hatred and your discontentment with your body and instead begin focusing it towards improving your wellbeing, learning to feel better in your skin. Finding a way of eating which makes you feel alive and nourished whilst changing habits and behaviours which will improve your energy and zest for life.

When you start to concentrate on wellbeing which is physical, emotional and spiritual and let the weight of your body take care of itself without trying to manipulate it in anyway, it will settle at a weight that is right for you personally. For some woman that may be up, down or it stays where it is, it may be permanent or temporary but none of which is even important for weight is no longer a reference to anything.

Emily: I'm healthy

....

One of my best friends has always been slimmer than me, always. For years I felt like the fat friend and compared my body to her body every time I saw her. Yet recently I've realised how, even though I've always been heavier than her, my health is far better than hers. She smokes and I don't. She drinks much more than I do. She's been under a significant amount of stress with her current employer which has really bothered her and affected her in so many ways emotionally. Recently she was diagnosed with a stomach ulcer perhaps stress related. It's really made me appreciate how my body size and my health are not as connected as I've always thought. Thin people get illnesses and diseases too.

According to Linda Bacon, author of 'Health At Every Size', she say that "HAES (Health at Every Size) is a holistic approach to self-acceptance that focuses on treating our bodies well and practicing acceptance of our own and others' bodies." As a side note, this approach is not limited to larger individuals. Eating disorders, food anxiety and body image issues can occur across a wide range of body sizes. Food issues and body insecurities don't discriminate, they can be present in anyone.

I truly believe that society needs to shift its focus from shame to support and from weight to wellbeing. Painting everyone with the same brush and casting the same assumptions is damaging and is failing members of our society as the ideology of if you're fat, lose some weight and if you're skinny, keep up the good work isn't helping anyone. I know from my time in practice that I've worked with clients who became food obsessed and compulsive eaters after incidents such as sexual assault and trauma, clients who binge in secret and no one has a clue what's going on and clients who may appear to be living a healthy lifestyle but are suffering from panic attacks and obsessive thoughts, so they aren't healthy anyway. What I'm saying is we can't make assumptions around health purely based on looking at someone's body! Truly understanding, listening and supporting someone in healing their relationship with food is all about helping them connect to the reasons why they eat like they do. It infuriates me when I hear other people recommending to stay away from the junk food and sugar laden snacks as a way of getting healthier and usually as a means of weight control. That's not ever going to work or address the root cause though if you don't know and appreciate what that junk food or sugar laden snack is doing for that person in the first place.

I believe that our emotional health plays a much more significant role in our overall health and wellbeing as far as I have experienced and witnessed, so let's focus on that part more than physically trying to lose weight in the belief that, in isolation, that will make you healthier. Weight loss is not the goal nor is it the focus. Your emotional and mental wellbeing is far more important than your waist size. Someone unhappy with their weight and body is more likely going to give up health and wellness focused activities than someone who is heavier yet satisfied and accepting of their size. Focussing on having a healthy body, mind and spirit when it comes from a place of love and kindness is always going to be better than coming from a place of hatred and negativity, the same way motivation to take care of your body and nurture her should come from your own place of self worth and not a beauty myth ideal. Interesting research from the University of New South Wales suggests that people who believe they are worthless as they aren't thin and who have tried and failed to lose weight, are significantly less likely to exercise than fat people who haven't internalised weight stigma. So dropping the weight stigma is vital. We are all more than a physical shape, age or any other number or label. Numbers don't define any of us and for that reason we can choose to get off the carousel of diets and self-hatred. We can choose to eat in a way which makes us feel energised and alive and we can choose to move our bodies because it makes us feel good and stronger by focusing on improving our wellbeing and quality of life. Not by doing any of that for the sole purpose of losing weight.

DIET CULTURE DOESN'T CARE ABOUT YOUR MENTAL HEALTH. I DO.

B.M.I - BULLSH*T, MISLEADING AND INACCURATE

B ody mass index (BMI), more properly Quetelet's index, was developed by Lambert Adolphe Jacques Quetelet who was a Belgian polymath and although it first appeared in his book On Man and the Development of His Faculties, or Essays on Social Physics in 1835, it wasn't until the late 1970s when BMI became more mainstream.

A few years ago my husband had a check up with the doctor and returned home fuming but also quite upset. His medical check had concluded that he was 'obese' and as a result had sat through a lecture from the nurse whilst she listed all the ailments he was now in danger of getting based on his BMI. She handed him a diet sheet disguised as a healthy eating plan and sent him on his way, telling him he needed to lose at least 8kg to bring his BMI down to a healthy range in order to reduce his chances of dying prematurely. As he threw the diet sheet on the kitchen counter and walked out of the room, I became aware of how frequently this happens throughout the world. I have lost count of the number of women who have reported a similar experience whilst tears have been streaming down their faces with fear in their eyes as they are told they are a ticking time bomb on the path towards heart disease, diabetes, high cholesterol and other ailments.

Instead of Body Mass Index, BMI should be renamed the Bullshit Mass Index as it is not a medically relevant scale as it provides no accurate description of anyone's overall health as we've just been discussing. As far as I am concerned, inaccuracy should never have a place in any medical protocol. Ever. In fact BMI produces a completely arbitrary number by simply dividing someone's weight by their height, yet that number has assigned to it so much meaning, especially through the eyes of the medical and health care profession.

My husband was obese according to his number and was in danger of illness and deteriorating health unless he dieted.

Yet he went to the gym 4 times a week.
Lifted weights 4 times a week.
Cycled hundreds of kilometres every week.
Had a resting heart rate and blood pressure well within the realms of normal
He didn't smoke
Slept soundly every night for at least 7-8 hours
Drank 2 litres of water every day
Drank alcohol only at the weekend and within the guidelines
Took supplements daily
Had a homeopath and other alternative health practitioners who he worked with
Had a job and business which brought him joy and happiness
Had a supportive and loving family unit where he felt loved, safe and appreciated.

Yet according to his BMI he needed to lose weight. None of the above was taken into account, just the number. Can you see how arbitrary that number is? It means nothing.

Incidentally a study published in the International Journal of Obesity reported that 'nearly 75 million adults in the US are misclassified as either healthy or unhealthy when BMI is used as the sole health indicator.' Not only that but since 2002 researchers kept discovering something in study after study what has now since been called the 'obesity paradox' where obese patients according to BMI with chronic diseases such as heart failure, diabetes, pneumonia, kidney disease and heart disease were shown to live longer and do better than those patients whose weight was 'normal' according to their BMI.

Interesting that isn't it?

Yet we do attach meaning to our BMI with many weight conscious, food obsessed individuals preoccupying their time with it, so concerned to make it smaller. This is where fat phobia plays a role.

Fat Shaming, Fat Phobia + The Fear Of Weight Gain

Our fear is not about gaining weight, it's the story we've attached to gaining weight.

We sadly live in a society which is fat phobic. A society which tells us that the cultural ideology of being slim is better than being fat. We have been conditioned that being fat is something which is inherently wrong and should be avoided at all costs. The medical profession tell us it will make us sick. Social media suggests we won't be happy without losing the weight and the marketers tell us that we don't belong if we don't wear those clothes, in those sizes and look a certain way whilst doing so.

We receive messages day in and day out of how the female body is supposed to look; tall, slim, blond, blemish free and more often than not white skinned. No wonder so many of us struggle to accept ourselves as we are.

I often delve into fat phobia with my clients and initially many seem perplexed with the topic, too afraid to admit that maybe they do have prejudice towards fat people. It's quite easy to find out whether you are fat phobic by answering this question. If you weren't afraid of gaining weight, would you still be concerned about your food choices?

Jenny: I hadn't even noticed

....

I hadn't realised I was exaggerating the negative impact of my food choices as I was actually suppressing fat phobia. I thought that choosing certain foods would stop me gaining weight which is so clearly fat phobic when I say it out loud!

Even reading this, there is likely a part of you worrying about 'what if I gain weight if I start following the advice she's giving?' I know you will be. Fear of weight gain is tied up in fat phobia, which is real. You are surrounded by it, some of it subtle and some of it not so much.

I want to address this one now, before we move on, as over the years I have seen this fear sneak up on women in a way which has sent them into a tail spin. After all, you have been calorie counting, weighing, measuring, tracking and controlling how and what you eat with the desire of losing weight or maintaining your weight for how many years? So how do we find that sweet spot between, 'I want to be a normal eater and no longer have these food and body struggles' with 'what if I gain weight?!'

FAT PHOBIA DRIVES WEIGHT OBSESSION

Firstly, you may have heard the term set point or perhaps you haven't. It's the theory that all bodies have a natural set point which, when we stop trying to manipulate them through food control, will be achieved. I'm only referencing it incase you might be curious where I stand with it but for me personally, I have no interest in theories or ideas about set points and what our bodies 'should' do when left to their own devices. Instead I'd rather focus on healing your food and weight obsession so that you can focus on nourishing yourself in a way which makes you feel good and without the guilt, shame and fear you have at the moment. Let's focus on dismantling your own fat phobia so it's no longer something which pulls you like an elastic band back into the world of diet culture. From that point you will by definition be more able to listen and allow your body to guide you to wherever she desires to go.

When we begin healing our relationship with food and our bodies, there is an adjustment period whilst we find our feet and learn to reconnect and tune back in (more coming on this), but eventually everything will settle down. It takes patience and a little practice but it will happen so acknowledge any fear which may be coming up for you, keep reading, keep exploring and make sure to use some of the tools in this book which you can get here: www.soulfedwoman.com/bookbonuses

Finally, your ability to intuitively feed yourself exactly what is right for you is a skill you were born with. However, you have lost that skill due to everything which we are talking about in this book. Dieting being one of the biggest. The good news is you can get it back as whatever you learn you can unlearn and then relearn.

EXERCISE

....

What meaning have you given to weight and body fat?

Think of a number or a size which, if you were to become, makes you feel anxious and fearful.

Now what do you think would happen to you, in your life, if you gained weight or became that size?

What beliefs and stories are coming up for you? (Fear of being judged, being unloveable, having failed, not being good enough, being rejected?)

All of those things are the REAL reasons why you are fearful of gaining weight. You've attached a meaning, emotion and story to weight gain, which naturally you want to avoid.

DIET CULT-URE

I never blame or judge those who participate in weight loss and diet culture. They are victims of a society that profits from their insecurities

Have you noticed how every single diet you have been on has, to some degree, brainwashed you to believing that their way is the best way?

Proteins are king
Carbs are evil
Fat is the devil
Sugar is the son of Satan!

They all create cult like attributes to their restrictive food movements, don't they?

You are weak if you give in to [insert whatever food you are not allowed]
You call it by name with many having a 'guru' heading the movement who is often worshipped and adored.
You live in fear of cheating or 'falling off the wagon' as each diet cult reinforces that sinning against the dietary deities is a reflection of our moral failing as a human being.
You feel triggered by how someone else chooses to eat, believing that your diet cult is the superior and the best.

It's funny how we rarely notice this whilst we subscribe to them, yet now I've brought that to your attention you can see it too, can't you?

So why are we swayed with the cult of dieting so easily and so often?

Diet cult-ure is the result of a fat phobic society which is bombarded with dieting propaganda centering around getting a 'bikini body' or 'beach body' and adding morality to food choices. Diet cult-ure tells us that all seven billion inhabitants on this planet should aspire to have the same socially acceptable body type and assumes that anyone who has wobbly bits must be fat and therefore needs fixing. For me though, diet cult-ure is the personification of all the rules which have told women that their only chance of happiness and living a fulfilled life is through shrinking. Shrinking your waist. Shrinking your body. Shrinking yourself. Shrinking your problems. Shrinking your mind. Shrinking your power.

DIET CULTURE DOESN'T WANT YOU TO BE A FULL PERSON IN SHAPE, INDIVIDUALITY OR INTELLECT. IT WANTS YOU TO SHRINK YOURSELF.

Besides giving us a communal topic which brings us together as women, the way we choose to eat also becomes part of our identity in which we become emotionally invested. Once you are in that mindset, you are continually looking for validation that the food rules you have adopted are true. Anyone with dysfunctional eating works really hard to maintain the beliefs they have around food as they think their rules are keeping them safe in some way and will do whatever they can to not break them. As you know though, we all break food rules as they are practically impossible to stick to forever. Yet despite all of this, the main reason we are swayed with the diet cults is our initial desire to lose weight. It's our desire to become slimmer, smaller and less of who we are. We, as a collective, crave weight loss.

EXERCISE: WHY DO YOU WANT TO LOSE WEIGHT?

....

List all of your reasons

How do you feel about what you wrote?

What does it bring up for you?

WHY WEIGHT LOSS WON'T FIX YOUR PROBLEMS

Picture the scene.

You wake up in the morning and tell yourself today is the day you will finally get your shit together and be good with food. No more binging. No more over eating. No more giving into the chocolate, the crips, the cake and whatever other 'bad' foods you find hard to resist.

You want to lose weight once and for all as you're sick and tired of feeling so rubbish about yourself, constantly beating yourself up and hating the way your body looks. You truly believe that if you were slimmer, more toned and 'good' with food that life would be less stressful than it is right now and you'd be feeling unstoppable in your skinny jeans and heels.

So what do you do?

What all too many of us have done. You strip off, have a wee and get a starting number from the scales in the bathroom. You kind of squint when reading the number as you have attached so much meaning to 'that' number. It represents your self worth. Your self esteem. How not 'enough' you are.

Feeling anxious and almost panicked that the number wasn't what you thought (it's gone up, again), you get dressed and go in the kitchen and start weighing, measuring, tracking and recording everything you eat from that point forward.

You tell yourself you can do it this time.

Once the weight comes off, this will all be worth it.

You psyche yourself up.
You tell everyone "I'm on a diet" or "I'm just being good with food"
You say 'no' to things.
You turn invitations down after all pizza restaurants aren't compatible with the diet and you convince yourself you weren't really bothered about going anyway.
You put your life on hold.
You stay focused, looking at the photo on the fridge or the image on your phone for motivation.
You keep reminding yourself of the goal while practicing affirmations whenever you feel your willpower slipping such as "I'm losing weight" and "I can do it this time!"

Sound familiar?

Listen gorgeous lady, I need to throw a huge bloody curve ball in the way you are choosing to think at the moment. Desiring to lose weight is not about feeling better about yourself. It's not about having more confidence. It's not about feeling more comfortable. It's not even about feeling happier.

Do you know what you are really buying into?

The idea that losing weight will fix your problems and will help you feel happier about life. Help you feel less stressed, less anxious and more accepted by society and by yourself. You'll become good enough.

So you keep 'trying' in the hope that one day you will find the willpower or find a diet which is easy to stick to and as if by magic you get given the key to the happy life door as soon as the number on the scale is the number you have attached happiness to.

I'm not saying this to be nasty or cruel but you will be waiting forever if you don't change how you are thinking.

There isn't a diet out there which will ever work, we're coming to the statistics soon, nor is there a key to a happy life door and there certainly isn't a switch that gets flicked as soon as you lose weight. I tried for 14 years to get to that place and several times when I did lose weight, my problems were still there, I wasn't any happier within myself and still didn't feel enough.

STOP FOCUSING ON YOUR WEIGHT AS BEING THE BARRIER TO YOUR HAPPINESS

Whenever we make our happiness be determined by our weight, we are deflecting what's really going on by blaming the size of our thighs, our tummies or the number on the scale we saw this morning in the bathroom. The truth being that right now, reading this book, you aren't happy or satisfied with life as it currently is which is completely OK to admit. However, losing 10lbs or 2 dress sizes won't fix those issues, problems or resolve your unhappiness. That takes a completely different approach.

WHAT I NOW KNOW ABOUT WEIGHT

The biggest lie that diet cult-ure sells us is that losing weight will make us happy. It won't. If you can't learn to love and accept your body, as she is, independent of shape, size, colour and anything else, you will never be happy as life doesn't change just because your jean size does and even if your jean size does change, the statistics say it won't last as dieting doesn't work in the long term.

Here are 6 things I now know about weight which I didn't when I was chasing slimness and fighting food cravings, over-eating and binge eating.

1. Happy life door ain't opening

We've just been talking about this but I feel it is such an important point to repeat. Despite what you might believe, I promise you that reducing your weight will not give you the key to the happy life door. Despite what we choose to think, life doesn't necessarily get 1000 times better when we come down in size because the satisfaction and contentment we get in life is not defined by the number on the scales, even though the diet industry wants us to believe otherwise. When I think about my own personal story, my slimmest points in that story were not my happiest and my happiest points were not my slimmest. I invite you to think about your story. Why do you attach so much emphasis and belief around losing weight = happiness. Where does that come from? Who told you that to be true?

2. Our weight does not determine our health.

We can be healthy at any size, any weight, any shape. There may be many people who disagree with this but I've seen it to be true and I believe it to be true. Someone who weighs less than someone else can be unhealthy and likewise, someone who weighs more to someone else can be healthy and vice versa.

3. Weight is not a direct reflection of our self worth.

Do you know what that number on the scales really is? It is just the numerical value of our gravitational pull on this planet in this body. Nothing more, nothing less. It's just a number. The value which we attach to that number is coming from within us based on our intrinsic values of self worth, self esteem and self acceptance. It comes from society, from diet culture, from the brainwashing that we, particularly as woman, have endured for years by climbing on and falling off diets. You are not your weight. You are so much more than your weight!

4. Drop the weight, change your focus

Giving up the need to control our weight can be challenging, difficult and uncomfortable at times, however, it's also the most freeing, rewarding, satisfying, liberating and empowering thing you can do for yourself and your future. Making peace with food and your body can be found by choosing to focus on different things. Moving away from weight as being the pivotal point of your life takes compassion, time & persistence of quietening down the diet voice in your head but it's possible. Completely possible.

5. Controlling weight is futile

Trying to control your physical weight, in a world where many things seem out of our control, creates a vicious cycle in which you can easily find yourself feeling stuck and trapped. Our lives cannot be controlled as our stories change, our lives evolve and our weight fluctuates depending on our cycles, our age and what's going on in life, so trying to control too much of that creates an internal battle field where we are constantly fighting ourselves. There is never a winner in that fight by the way, just more upset, frustration, feeling even more inadequate and turning to food to make yourself feel better.

6. It's ok to take up space!

Trying to shrink ourselves in order to take up less space in the world is not ok. History shows how women have been systemically suppressed to be less of themselves, to be quiet, to take a back seat, to not be allowed to follow their dreams or own their desires. Yet that was then and this is now. Forcing your amazing body to become less through weight control, is just another way of reenforcing that it's not ok to take up space as yourself and that's simply not true. You are enough just how you are and you are deserving and worthy of taking up as much space in your own life as you bloody well want to.

Right then gorgeous, let's keep going. I want to explore the world of dieting with you next. This is a juicy one.

WHAT ARE DIETS?

We often think we are addicted to food, but actually we are addicted to dieting and the drama it ensues as weight control is the addiction

When dieting, each calorie and each food choice has the power to make or break your day. Each bite you take or don't take feels like the difference between you being good or bad. Winning or failing at life. With dieting, it feels like each pound you lose or gain defines your week, your self worth and your level of allowed happiness. Diets, dieting and food restriction all contribute towards dysfunctional eating, such as emotional eating and bingeing in such a significant way, that we're going to explore this in much more detail now.

The definition of a diet according to the dictionary is this:

"a special course of food to which a person restricts themselves, either to lose weight or for medical reasons"

Despite the different names, ideology and branding, all diets are very much the same.

They involve rules of some description.
They involve some sense of restriction and deprivation.
They always place invisible labels on food by categorising them as either good and bad and they always turn food choice and eating into a moral issue.

I asked my community a little while ago what dieting meant to them. Here are some of the answers they gave:

'restriction, hard work, depression, deprivation, stressful, overwhelm, failure, losing control, feeling bad, snappy, miserable'

Sounds delightful. Remind me why we do this to ourselves again?

Now it could be that you are reading this and thinking, 'but I'm not on a diet, I just want to know how to not be so obsessed about food and my body.'

Many people believe they are not dieting as they don't follow a certain plan. They don't go to weekly diet club meetings, they don't buy diet books and they don't measure or track what they eat, yet their way of interacting with food is very much likened to being on a diet. This is what I call diet mentality.

Diet mentality is when we think like a dieter, so we order side salad inside of fries, we choose a skinny latte rather than full fat and we go for the low fat or fat free salad dressing as it's the 'healthier option.' You do not have to be on a conventional diet to be emotionally attached to food choice. As soon as you are attached in that way, you have unintentionally added morality to the conversation believing that the slice of chocolate cake you just ate was bad, therefore you must be bad too. That thought process is exactly the same as someone following a diet plan who falls off the wagon.

DIETS ARE ANY KIND OF EMOTIONAL ATTACHMENT TO THE WAY WE ARE CHOOSING TO EAT.

So why do we eat with attachment? Why do we view the choices we make with food as being an indicator of our mortality as a human being?

It's our desire to lose weight again.

The desire to lose weight is preventing you from eating without attachment.

I'm hoping you can appreciate why we need to talk about diets and wanting to lose weight in order for you to truly overcome food obsession, binge eating and emotional eating? The more you diet, the more significant your chances of bingeing, overeating and food obsession so actually one could argue that dieting creates the very issues which you are wanting to overcome in the first place!

AS LONG AS WE WANT TO LOSE WEIGHT, WE WILL NEVER BE FREE TO TRUST OURSELVES WITH FOOD OR TRUST OUR BODIES WHEN IT COMES TO FOOD CHOICE.

So tell me, when did you start dieting, either on a conventional diet or by way of becoming emotionally attached to how you eat, such as viewing carbs as being bad?

Teens is a very common age for dieting to grab us tightly in its grasp as our body is changing with puberty and our emotional intelligence and identity is evolving as we start to figure out who we are and where we fit in to the world around us. During this time we can often feel out of control with our bodies and our emotions, not to mention the increasing pressure we find ourselves under. It is the time when social pressures far outweigh family opinion and when we frequently compare our physical and intellectual self to our counterparts within school. This time of my life was challenging as it was for so many women within our community, and my adventure into the world of dieting started around this time too which is no coincidence. Yet horrifying research shows the age of first time dieters is falling. They are getting younger.

A study by Common Sense Media in 2015 hit the headlines when it reported that 80% of 10 year old girls have been on a diet. In 1970 the average age for a girl dieting was 14 according to The Eating Disorder Foundation yet by 1990, the average age had dropped to eight years old and that number hasn't changed. Look at some of the diet industry's market leaders, you can see how younger members are welcomed. Weight Watchers allows children as young as 10 to join its program, Slimming World has a special plan just for children aged 11-15 (which is free if they attend with a paying member, so mother and daughter can do it together), Jenny Craig is 13 and Nutrisystem is 14 and I believe it's at the discretion of the company to allow younger children in, especially when supported by a medical or healthcare professional. I recently heard of a 6 year old child going to a very well known diet club here in the UK. These numbers are shocking aren't they? Anyone who doesn't think that children are being psychologically harmed by diet culture are either turning a blind eye or ignoring the facts which are glaringly obvious.

ERIKA: DIETING AT 8 YEARS OLD

....

My mum put me on a well known diet plan and gave me shakes to drink when I was 8 and it messed me up. Looking at photos I was a normal weight, a little chubby, but certainly not needing to diet. I was so self conscious of my body which was made worse by my parents not allowing me to have a normal relationship with food. Mum used to say I'd get fat if I ate too much and dad used to tell me 'you don't need to eat that' as they were both worried I'd get fat. I rebelled when I got older as they couldn't stop me anymore and I've been fighting my body and food ever since. I have binge eating disorder and I'm the heaviest I've ever been.

Erika isn't an exception, I've heard so many similar stories it still brings me to tears thinking of these little children being put on diets and being taught they can't trust their bodies and subconsciously starting to feel they aren't accepted in society or even by their families unless they slim down and change who they are.

EXERCISE: HOW EXPERIENCED AT DIET-ING ARE YOU?

....

Take a look at these common and not so common weight loss and diet programs. I'd like you to award yourself one point for each one that you have been on at some point in your life and keep a record of that number as you go through the list:

Weight Watchers
Atkins
Dukan
South Beach
5:2
Cambridge
Slimming World
3 hour diet
Slimfast
LighterLife
Herbalife
Rosemary Connelly
Cabbage Soup
Grapefruit
Caveman diet
Fat Flush
French women don't get fat
GI diet
NutriSystem
Macrobiotic
Volumetric diet

Cayenne Pepper+ Maple Syrup
Juice Fast
Juice+
Master Cleanse
Keto
Alkaline
Blood Type
Jenny Craig
Low fat
Mediterranean
Paleo
Gluten free
The Zone
Raw foodism

What was your total number?
Was it higher or lower than you thought?
How do you feel about the number that you have?
Does that shock you, surprise you or upset you?

When Healthy Eating Turns Harmful

As she walked into the consulting room, her skin was tinged with orange. I thought it was badly applied make up at first until she came closer, shook hands and sat down.

'How can I help you?' I asked as she placed her slim frame in the chair opposite my desk.

Jessie was 32 and very health conscious, to the point of obsession. Her periods had become irregular, she was suffering from bouts of insomnia, anxiety and heart palpitations and she was now wanting help with it all. It was clear in speaking with her that she wasn't in a good place, emotionally and physically. I suspected that she was in the throes of a potentially serious disorder called orthorexia. She thought the same. Jessie only ate pure, clean and healthy food, much of which was raw vegan, and that orange tinge wasn't badly applied make up as I had initially thought, it was in fact from the carrots and sweet potatoes she consumed several times a day.

Jessie isn't alone. More and more people are falling into this category of becoming orthorexic without fully appreciating the severity of their perfectionism and obsession when it comes to 'healthy' food. I hid my dysfunctional eating and desire for slimness behind healthy eating for quite some time. Weighing out nutrient dense foods, eating sugar free and super clean replaced all the diet plans as I convinced myself I was doing it for the good of my body and my overall health. Yet that didn't stop me jumping on the scales everyday and fighting the food cravings and urge to eat normally which increased the healthier I ate.

The term 'orthorexia' was coined in 1998 and refers to an obsession with proper or 'healthy' eating. Although being concerned and aware of the nutritional quality of the food we eat isn't a problem in and of itself, someone with orthorexia becomes so fixated on so-called 'healthy eating' that they actually damage their own well-being as it effects their mental health and day to day living.

Here are some signs of orthorexia which I've seen in my practice as per The National Eating Disorder's website:

- Compulsive checking of ingredient lists and nutritional labels

- An increase in concern about the health of ingredients

- Cutting out an increasing number of food groups (all sugar, all carbs, all dairy, all meat, all animal products)

- An inability to eat anything but a narrow group of foods that are deemed 'healthy' or 'pure'

- Unusual interest in the health of what others are eating

- Spending hours per day thinking about what food might be served at upcoming events

- Showing high levels of distress when 'safe' or 'healthy' foods aren't available

- Obsessive following of food and 'healthy lifestyle' blogs on social media

Perfectionism with eating is around us all the time. Next time you scroll through instagram, see how many photos of smoothie bowls, raw food salads and Buddha bowls you notice which, as I've said, there isn't anything necessarily wrong with them, but you can't help agree that such images could potentially reinforce this desire for ultimate healthy eating in someone sensitive to that way of thinking, all of which has the danger of normalising what is actually a really unhealthy relationship and response to food.

Intuitive eating or mindful eating is another one which many of my clients have followed at some point on their dieting journey. I've witnessed diet obsessed individuals move away from conventional dieting towards intuitive eating and simply replaced one set of rules with another which defeats the entire point of finding your freedom. It's so easy to turn intuitive eating in to yet another way of gauging how well or bad you're doing as you find yourself munching on something only to realise you weren't physically hungry and then get frustrated with yourself for doing so! The same can be said for Paleo and Intermittent Fasting as despite them being masked as a way of eating to improve health, they still are very much a diet at the end of the day for they have rules which shouldn't be broken. Also don't be fooled but the 'it's a lifestyle' label. Lifestyle is the new name for 'diet' which many people end up taking a break from or falling off once in a while, proving that diets in disguise are out there.

JAN: SPORT FANATIC

....

I went from over 200 pounds down to 130 by dieting and working out at least 5 times per week. I had so many people complimenting me and telling me how inspirational I was and I must admit, I lived for that validation at the time. I trained to run a half marathon after getting the running bug, but it wasn't necessarily for the pleasure or exhilaration, it was for the calories I could burn the longer I was able to run for. At the time of running it, I looked incredible. I had become that woman in the gym all the time, telling myself that exercise was good for my body and receiving admiration from fellow gym members and trainers on how well I was doing. Yet I'd become obsessed about my appearance, I was having compulsive and dysmorphic thoughts about the way I looked and I started binging then purging through exercise. I ultimately gained all the weight back. I now know that my healthy lifestyle was hiding some very deep rooted beliefs about my feelings of inadequacy and dieting actually made things 10x worse. I've learnt to embrace and start showing myself kindness over recent months, instead of beating my body into submission. It's the only way forward.

Over recent years some of the diet industry's market leaders have tried to reposition themselves as being a program which teaches their members (or customers) how to lead a healthy lifestyle but I beg to differ. There are plenty of them which do it in such a way that even though they claim it's about education and living a healthy lifestyle, you never really have full freedom over what you're choosing to put into your body. Becoming obsessed with 'points' or tracking your 'Syns' won't ever teach you how to live healthily, it will simply force you to rely on them, so you keep paying your monthly subscription, buying their low fat cake (which isn't cake), and remain woefully uneducated and disconnected from what your body actually needs whilst believing that you cannot trust yourself around food choices without said system being in place. It disempowers people to not listen to themselves. It teaches people that their bodies cannot be trusted whilst reinforcing the idea that food needs to be monitored.

So here's a question for you? When did it become so important for any of us to label how we eat, to systemise our eating process and to turn it all into a moral conversation? Eating and food choice should be one of the most natural and uncomplicated things we do as human beings yet there are literally millions of people in all corners of the globe who find this far from natural. You're probably one of them.

A side note about food allergies and ailments

If you have been diagnosed with food allergies or a health condition where food choice needs to be monitored, this goes without saying that these 'rules' are for your highest and greatest good as they are not restricting but rather helping and assisting you to feel good in your body. Ailments like Celiac disease, diverticulitis, Crohn's and colitis along with inflammatory conditions such as arthritis benefit from making food choices in the best interest of feeling good. I worked as a nutritionist therapist for several years and it is completely possible to embrace food rules through empowerment which are in the interest of your wellbeing whilst still finding your food freedom. It starts with choice and reframing any thoughts which make you feel restricted. You are free to eat bread whenever you like but if your body has celiac disease, she will feel pretty poorly afterwards. It's still a choice though. The more you take your power back and choose to nourish your body based on feeling good and improving your well being, the easier any health imposed food rules are to navigate.

THE MINNESOTA STARVATION EXPERIMENT

You would be forgiven if you hadn't heard of the Minnesota starvation experiment, neither had I until several years ago. Yet this discovery helped me to get a real understanding of why I had struggled and fought for years to get my binging, over eating and yo yo dieting under control.

During World War II, conscientious objectors in the US and the UK were asked to volunteer for medical research, known as the Minnesota Starvation Experiment. The young men volunteers were starved and monitored for six months to help experts decide how to treat victims of mass starvation. All over Europe people were starving - in the Netherlands, in Greece, in eastern Europe and the Soviet Union - and the US military wanted to learn how best to re-feed them. But first they had to find healthy people willing to be starved.

This clinical study was performed at the University of Minnesota and started in November 1944 and for the first three months the participants were fed to their optimum weight and monitored. Then their rations were cut dramatically.

This experiment was tough, super tough. Not only was food rationed but they were also put through extreme exercise in order for their bodies to be running on a deficit and to ultimately get into the state of starvation. It was quite horrendous really. Now the fascinating part of the experiment was more about the emotional and psychological impact that starvation had on these previously healthy men, something which the original experiment had not expected. This is where it gets interesting for you.

FOOD QUICKLY BECAME AN OBSESSION.

Some volunteers reported being fixated on food and the idea of eating. Dreaming about food, thinking about food to the point of obsession. They found themselves reading cookbooks and trying to get their hands on anything which was food related. In addition throughout the 6 months, a high percentage of the men reported feeling numb, feeling disconnected from their bodies, not feeling pain and losing all sexual desires. Anxiety and depression were also widely recorded within the volunteers and some recorded eating illicit food before becoming despondent with guilt.

Although its original intention was not focused on the psychological implications of starvation, this study has since become a source of reference for eating disorder recovery centres as it reflects something which you and I are all too familiar with.

Dieting!

Although most of us never have gotten to the extremes which this experiment did, the similarities are striking to that of a compulsive and chronic dieter.

Restriction. Food obsession. Guilt. Obsessive thoughts. Numbness. Anxiety. Depression.

How many of those things have you experienced?

WHEN YOU REMOVE AND RESTRICT FOOD, YOU BECOME PSYCHOLOGICALLY CHALLENGED AROUND FOOD. THE LONGER THE RESTRICTION, THE WORST THE OBSESSION BECOMES. THE LONGER YOU DIET, THE MORE PRONE YOU ARE TO BECOME FOOD OBSESSED.

THE EXPLOITATION AND PROFIT OF THE DIET INDUSTRY

Many of my clients have spent hours critiquing their bodies, hating how they look, disliking their legs, they find their cellulite revolting and they can't bear to look at themselves naked. They want it all gone and sometimes take drastic measures to lose the fat.

Can you imagine if every single woman woke up tomorrow feeling more confident, happier and more comfortable with who she was without wanting to diet or lose weight? Just think how many businesses, organisations and companies would go out of business. How much money would be lost, not just in the diet industry but throughout other industries whose bank balances are filled through our body insecurities and wanting to change our appearances - think cosmetic surgery, makeup, clothes, slimming pills, hair dye, hair extensions, nails, eye lashes and fake tan. The list is endless!

Think about it. There are companies who sell us anti cellulite creams, products to help smooth our skin, things you can buy to change your hair along with make up and beauty products to help you look blemish free. There are garments which help smooth away our lumps, bumps and wobbly bits, as heaven forbid they are ever on show to the world (gasp). You can spend a fortune whilst a beautician uses a futuristic gadget to tighten skin and tone your legs whilst lotions, potions, creams and products all exploit how we feel about the body we are living in. What about all the treatments available which claim they can freeze fat, sculpt fat or melt away fat by being wrapped like a turkey in clingfilm? I once spent £1000 or $1300(!) on oxygen fat burning therapy. I sat in an oxygen infused tank for 20 minutes before dressing in a plastic gym suit to perform 40 minutes of exercises as I sweated profusely in an overheated room. I was also advised to cut carbs and only eat protein, fruit and vegetables for the duration of the treatment which guaranteed weight loss (starvation would do that though, right?!)

Although I am incredibly embarrassed to admit this to you, the sadness I feel about it now is real as I wasn't the only woman in that place. The room was filled with other desperate women whose flushed faces were peeking out of the oxygen tanks and who too hadn't seen that we'd all been ripped off. I didn't get the results I was promised by the way. Any weight loss which was recorded at the end of my session was due to extreme water loss and dehydration through sweating which always returned once I drank enough water!

Yet despite these other services and offerings, it's safe to say that the diet industry is categorically the leader of them all.

The word 'diet' first appeared in English in the 13th century and its meaning was the same as modern English 'habitually consumed food and drink.' Yet during the Middle and modern English periods, it began to mean a 'way of living' in particular a way of living as prescribed by a physician or regime. From the quotations cited by the Oxford English Dictionary, it's clear that "diet" was often used to refer to a regime in prisons – as in "bread and water diet" - interesting that the link between "dieting" and "deprivation" or "punishment" is still present in many people's minds today.

So even though the word 'diet' was being used as far back as the 13th century, how on earth did the diet industry become the monster that we now know it to be?

Looking through the history books, we can see that weight started to inch its way into the awareness of the USA around the turn of the 20th century and as weighing scales became more affordable and accurate, it was during this time that doctors started to routinely record their patient's height and weight at every visit, for no other reason except they now had the technology to do so. Whilst writing this book, I came across a book from 102 years ago from 1916 by Amelia Summerville called 'Why Be Fat? Rules for Weight Reduction and the Preservation of Youth and Health' in which she writes 'I would rather die than be fat.' So even at the turn of the 20th century, society was already starting to become aware of thinness and fatness and how one was superior to the other.

With the advancement of medicine and pharmaceuticals, we also know that by the 1920s weight loss drugs were mainstream with doctors often prescribing thyroid medication to healthy people to make them slimmer. Jump forward another decade and by the 1930s 2,4-dinitrophenol or DNP came along. This was a highly toxic industrial chemical mainly used as a pesticide but was bizarrely found to promote rapid weight loss in humans when they ingested it although it was banned by the FDA in 1938 because of serious adverse reactions, one of which was death. Amphetamines, laxatives and diuretics swiftly followed, all of which carried with them side effects ranging from nausea and dizziness to more serious ones which sometimes were fatal.

This growing national obsession of weight increased further in 1942 when the Metropolitan Life Insurance Company created desirable height and weight charts for its policy holders. Literally overnight, people and their doctors were able to compare their bodies to the standardised notion of what was 'normal' or what they 'should' weigh based on these charts. Language started to shift and words which had previously been used such as plump or chubby were now replaced by more clinical sounding words such as overweight and obese. Just out of interest the word overweight implies that someone is over the 'correct' or 'right' weight they should be whilst obese comes from the Latin 'obesus' meaning 'having eaten until fat'. Both of these words convey a significant moral judgement when used based on their meanings, yet these are words which are freely used nowadays often within the medical field.

Speaking of which, in 1949 The National Obesity Society was created by a small group of doctors who believed that any level of thinness would be healthier than being fat. Not only was this the first of many professional associations which later formed all in a bid to take obesity treatment from the minority to the masses, but it was the start of a shift in attitude of obesity treatment creation including horrific ones like jaw wiring and stereotactic brain surgery that burned lesions into the hypothalamus.....all in a quest for slimness.

During these times it can be accurately assumed that people in the medical profession and many working professionals who were instrumental in being the catalysts for the diet industry to grow in to what it is today would have been men, not women. Women were very much home makers during the first half of the 20th century. So could we say that the diet industry was created by men based on their beliefs of what a 'normal' body should look like and weigh during a time when women were treated significantly unequal to men? How does that make you feel? Anyway I digress, let's continue.

Our modern diet industry is not just diet plans though, it's also made up of medical procedures. Bariatric surgeries are the most common of modern day treatment (and I use the word treatment very loosely) and it's big business, pardon the unintended pun. Hospital facilities resembling 5 star hotels serve up menus for their patients to select from; gastric band, gastric bypass, gastric balloon or a gastric sleeve, the choice is yours! These types of surgeries shockingly have increased from 37,000 being performed in the USA in 2000 to 220,000 by 2013…and not only does that number continue to grow but the age of the patients is falling. Obese children as young as 14 are undergoing weight-loss surgery in the UK on the NHS and although these cases are an exception, they are happening. The statistics around this topic are overwhelming and I completely understand the desire to help these children but removing parts of their stomach is not the answer. For anyone who is resorting to weight loss surgery, you have to question why they are where they are. You have to question whether what they really need is to heal their relationship with food and understand why they eat like they do as they are using it for so many reasons other than to satisfy physical hunger. Something isn't right. The side effects of having your stomach stapled, bypassed or part of it cut out and thrown in a bin, are not to be laughed at. Complications can include long-term malnutrition, intestinal blockages, disordered eating and even death. I have personally worked with several post-bariatric surgery patients and their stories have been heart breaking.

CAMILLA: BINGE EATING POST SURGERY

....

I took the decision to have a gastric band in 2013 after years of struggling with my weight. I thought it would be the answer to everything. The surgeon ran through the possible complications but seemed sure it would really help me get my weight and eating under control. I felt great for the first few weeks after the surgery even though I could only drink soup through a straw, it was when I was allowed to start eating food again that everything changed. I had tummy ache quite a lot and whenever I ate I had reflux as the contents of my stomach felt like it was coming back up.

Even though I did lose weight initially quite quickly, after a few months it slowed down and the desire to over ride the band became obsessive, I just wanted to eat. Someone had physically shrunk my stomach but nothing had changed in my head. I still had food cravings, I still felt compelled to binge but found it harder because of the surgery. That's when I found ways of satisfying the compulsion by eating tubs of ice cream which melted quickly and took up less space as well as drinking melted chocolate, pretty much anything which was in liquid form as my gastric band allowed me to eat that easier. I was already in a bad place with food and myself prior to my surgery but I can honestly say that the gastric band surgery amplified my food obsession significantly. It made everything worse.

Camilla was one of the lucky ones as her procedure was reversible. She had her gastric band removed and we worked together on healing her relationship with food once and for all. Yet for those patients who have parts of their stomach thrown into the bin in the operating room, life will never be the same again.

IRRELEVANT OF WHAT THEIR PRODUCT, PROGRAM OR MERCHANDISE, THE DIET INDUSTRY SELLS US ONE THING..... ......THAT SLIMNESS EQUALS HAPPINESS. THEY DO THIS BY BODY SHAMING US TO BUY FROM THEM.

I'm sure that you are all too familiar with the crazy fad diets which have existed over the years and more than likely tried your fair share, yet some have been actually quite shocking. From the tapeworm diet were individuals were fed parasites in the belief that they absorbed nutrients from their intestines resulting in weight loss, to the sleeping beauty diet where individuals fasted under sedation, people have resorted to drastic measures in a quest to slim down. Even the cigarette industry marketed itself not too long ago as helping you lose weight which, thankfully we now no longer believe.

The marketers behind the diet industry are arguably top of their game with many organisations throwing huge amounts of money into market research so they know their customers inside and out. They know you. They know what you like. What you don't. They know all about your struggles, low self-esteem and self worth. They know all about your desires to be slim and how much emotion you've attached to your dream weight. They know how desperate and confused you are when it comes to your acceptance of your body as it is. And it's these exact pain points which are fully exploited for their marketing campaigns.

Without even naming any of the diet industry giants, think about any marketing connected with them and their brand and you'll notice that the images are very suggestive whilst being subliminal. It's not uncommon to see images of a smiling woman, throwing her hair back whilst laughing and drinking coffee or a glass of wine with her friends in a socially acceptable slim body printed all over flyers or in magazine adverts. What message is this giving out? What do we start to believe? What do these deliberate choices of imaginary suggest? They imply in order to be content and happy in life, slimness is a prerequisite. We start to be pulled towards believing that without following a certain program or buying into an eating plan, that we will never be as happy, content and smily as the lady staring up at us from the advertisement.

So why do we buy into this? Why do we have this deep ingrained belief that in order to be happy, content and perhaps even feel worthy, lovable and accepted, our bodies need to be slim? And why are we so easily convinced we need the services which the diet and weight loss industry are creating for us. Notice I said 'services' and not 'solutions? That was deliberate.

We've already mentioned fat phobia and here it is again. It's real. Very real. Society has become so fat phobic there is a true fear for many women of becoming fat, you only need to take a look at some of the previous topics we've been discussing. We have an opinion of fat people. We believe that being slim is somehow better than being fat. We think that a slimmer and smaller body is more desirable than a larger and fatter body. And it's because of this undeniable fat phobia and fat shaming that the diet industry will never run out of customers. And that's what we are. Customers. Numbers on a profit and loss account reflecting their annual turnover.

In fact, if you step back and take an eagle eye view, you'll start to witness and observe how fat phobia is being fed (pun intended) by the diet industry itself! Not only is the diet industry breeding this increasing phobic response to fatness through its 'slim' focused marketing campaigns, they are also exploiting it and turning more people into paying customers.

DIET CULTURE ISN'T ABOUT YOU OR ME OR WHAT WE NEED. IT'S A BUSINESS. AND A TERRIFYINGLY SMART ONE AT THAT.

At the end of the day the diet industry is all about exploitation and profit, selling people something which won't give them what they want for diets don't work and slimness does not equal happiness. Instead it gives the companies selling them a very healthy profit margin along with happy shareholders.

How do you feel that your body insecurities are being exploited to make other people money? How do you feel that your self-esteem and self worth is being used as a tool to sell you something under the false illusion that when you use it, join it or follow it, your body will not only become slimmer but all your problems will miraculously disappear and life will be brighter, happier and filled with rainbows, unicorns and fairy dust? How do you feel? Angry? Upset? Pissed off? You've got every reason to feel all of those things…..and we're just getting started.

DIET STATISTICS

You probably don't need me to tell you that dieting can become a full time job for many. If you aren't on one, you are preparing to start one and when you start one you are trying your best to stay on it! And we do this for years....and years....and years.

According to a survey done in 2017 by Alpro which surveyed 2,000 people, they found that the average dieter follows 55 fad diets during their lifetime at a staggering cost of £30,000 or $40,000, which highlights more than just the financial cost of dieting but also how much time we lose to dieting. The average woman spends 17 years of her life dieting according to the statistics (I would argue it's much higher) and will go on between 4 and 5 diets every year. Another survey of more than 2,000 UK adults conducted by Mintel in 2016 uncovered that almost two thirds of women (57%) had tried to lose weight in the previous year, which suggests that nearly two thirds of women are dieting.

Yet it's our American cousins who spend more money on dieting, dieting products and weight loss surgery than any other people in the world, which in 2016 was an amount to the tune of £51 BILLION or $66.3 BILLION. This included weight loss programs, diet clubs, diet soda, weight loss drugs, weight loss surgeries, meal replacements, diet food and that number is growing each year. That's a lot of people whose body insecurities and feelings of inadequacy are making huge sums of money for a lot of businesses and much of it is happening on our own doorsteps. Market leaders of the diet world dominate the church and community halls throughout our towns and villages, with the average customer spending around £1200 or $1500 a year on their own branded products such as branded foods, classes, books, magazines and subscriptions.

The world's biggest and most popular diet business is currently Weight Watchers which operates in 30 countries across the globe. According to their fiscal report of 2016 they had 2.6 million subscribers worldwide which grew 22.6% by the end of 2017, adding roughly 600,000 new members from the same time a year earlier. In 2017, they snagged £1 billion or $1.307 billion in sales which was up 12% from the same time a year earlier and since getting celebrities on board with their brand such as Oprah who holds a 10% stake and more recently Dj Khaled, looking ahead, the company said it expects full-year 2018 revenue to approach £1.2 billion or $1.55 BILLION.

Just let those numbers sink in for a moment.

Most of us have been a member of such a group at some point on our weight loss journey.

Perhaps even more than once. I know I did. Every time I went back I'd tell myself I could do it this time yet the same thing always happened. It's this returning customer which the diet industry relies upon.

THE WEIGHT LOSS INDUSTRY THRIVES ON FAILURE. IF PEOPLE DIDN'T KEEP COMING BACK, THEY WOULDN'T HAVE A BUSINESS.

Richard Samber, former finance director of Weight Watchers from 1968-1993, was quoted as saying if a person cannot maintain their weight loss then they will keep returning to the company.

"That's where your business comes from".

Shocked? I'm not. I've studied dieting and eating psychology for years now and time and time again evidence and research shows that diets don't work, yet the people buying into them keep hoping that one day they'll find the diet which does work for them. In the meantime they keep paying, hoping and believing the empty promises the diet industry sells them, the whole while blaming themselves when the number on the scale doesn't change and wondering why their relationship with food is becoming more chaotic the harder they try to stay on plan.

A study published in the Journal of Adolescent health 2012 concluded that dieters were two to three times more likely than non-dieters to develop binge eating problems. I personally know my binge eating worsened as my diet addiction did. In fact I can say there was a direct correlation between the two although it wasn't apparent to me at the time as I didn't know what I didn't know back them. Many of my clients have said the same. On a similar note another study from the University of Colorado showed that 35 percent of people who start dieting can become addicted to dieting! And it is addictive isn't it? I often say dieting is like a drug and when we turn our backs on diets we can feel uncomfortable for a little while. Dieting is so culturally and sociologically accepted, it can be challenging to not be enticed back to diet culture for weight control is addictive.

So let's talk numbers and results shall we? What about success rates? It's surprisingly pretty hard to find concrete evidence and proof of the long term success rates of diets for many studies and research measure success by weight coming down initially, which arguably would happen for anyone who started controlling food, but what about staying down? The best data we have says that at least 95% regain some or more weight within 3-5 years of losing it. Some studies even suggest that long term success of dieting is as low as 0.01%, meaning out of 1000 people, only one person would have permanent (5 years or more) weight loss success through dieting.

Or in other words diets could be seen to have a failure rate of 99.9%

Now I haven't done statistics since my maths A levels but I know enough to say that's a rubbish prognosis for putting yourself through weeks and months of deprivation, restriction and feeling grumpy. Isn't it?

If we reframed it by saying an airline only had a success rate of 0.01% of arriving at the destination it's promising before we embark....would you still get on that plane? Knowing there was a 99.9% chance of it never getting to the place you think it's heading? Of course not! And if for some reason you did, would you blame yourself or the airline for misleading you when it arrived at a completely different location from the one printed on your boarding card? Hopefully you'd point the blame at the airline for deceiving you in the first place. Yet we never question the airline, the diet, the vessel, as being at fault. We blame ourselves instead and our lack of willpower or discipline.

Enough gorgeous one!

Diets are statistically shown to fail from the outset and for those who miraculously are in the minority and manage to maintain their new weight, this is a full time obsession of a different kind.

JANIE: I STOPPED LIVING

....

I maintained my 30lb weight loss for 6 years by calorie counting everything I ate and exercising pretty much every day. I had to try and manage the intrusive thoughts and being so preoccupied and obsessed with food that it took so much energy, time and discipline. I stopped living. I was in constant fear of the weight going back on that it took over. I often questioned what was I even doing it for.

And this isn't uncommon. People who maintain their weight loss in the long term do so as it becomes their top priority or obsession and this isn't a desirable way to live.

Let's be clear about one thing, regardless of what name they have, all the diet brands which dominate the weight loss industry are businesses at the end of the day and all businesses in any industry focus their attention on making as much profit as possible by finding new and inventive ways of repackaging and recreating themselves in the hope of attracting their ideal customers. You.

Such industry leaders spend an exorbitant amount of money every year researching and marketing to their ideal target market so as to use this information to grow their business to the next billion dollar mark through celebrity endorsements and rebranding. Although market research is obviously needed in any industry, the problem which I have in this regard, is that the needs of their ideal customers are not being met or even addressed. Actually they aren't even coming close. Let me explain.

Think of a diet club you have been a member of or a program you are bought in to. You have signed up with them because you want to lose weight. You want to be thinner. You want to feel more confident about your body. These are the pain points which all of their marketing is aimed and directed at. Nothing wrong in that I hear you say. However, on closer inspection and particularly as you are reading this book right now, how often has that outcome materialised? Permanent weight loss? I'll give you a moment to think about it.

Your desire for slimness has been elusive. Your desperation to slim down has either never happened or it's happened temporarily and then your weight has gone back up again. Feeling more confident in your body may also never have improved permanently and it's because these programs are not designed to give you what you actually need which is healing your relationship with food and improving your body image. That would arguably be the worst business model in the world, for if somebody were to heal their relationship with their body permanently, they would no longer go to the weekly weigh in meetings, spend their money on merchandise or in fact be a customer. Like I said, not the ideal business model to grow into a global force within the diet industry market place.

On our first session Zara was naturally defensive about dieting being to blame for her food and weight obsession. What came out of her mouth I have heard a hundred times over. 'Dieting works for me though. I lost 2 stone with a well known diet club in the UK a few years ago but then life got busy and I stopped going to meetings and tracking my food and my weight crept back up again. It does work though, it worked for me.'

'No it didn't. If it did you wouldn't have put all the weight back on with extra and you and I wouldn't be here having this conversation.' I could see by the look in her eyes that the penny dropped.

IF THEIR CUSTOMERS WERE GIVEN EVERYTHING WHICH THEY TRULY NEEDED THEY WOULD NO LONGER NEED TO BE CUSTOMERS AND THAT WOULDN'T MAKE FOR HAPPY SHAREHOLDERS

About 2 years I had the privilege of working with a lovely client called Catherine (not her real name.) Now Catherine's story was very typical of somebody who had struggled for a lifetime with food, eating and with her body. Yet the fascinating part of Catherine's story was that she was a weight loss consultant with one of the biggest brands in the UK. She lead up to 6 classes a week in her local area, teaching men and women how to lose weight based on the brand which she was a representative for. Starting our time together was difficult for her as she had so much shame that she had needed to approach me in the first place.

Whilst we were working together she revealed that since she became a part-time consultant with her diet brand, her own personal struggles with food had amplified. She had found herself frequently feeling like a fraud as she was bingeing in secret and hiding her dysfunctional relationship with food to all of her group members. She told me many of her colleagues struggled with food and eating themselves as they openly talked about it with each other behind closed doors and away from their groups.

Weight loss consultants such as Catherine are brand loyal followers who will defend their company much like fans do with their favourite celebrities or football teams. Yet they too can find themselves becoming trapped in a cognitive bias where everything revolves around the brand whilst ignoring what their customers actually need. By her own admission, Catherine told me that all the consultants who represent the brand are trained by that company to be, in effect, a sales team with minimal training given on nutrition, health and other topics which one would assume might be important for people in those positions. They use language which represents the company products knowing how to optimise the amount spent per group member by encouraging them to purchase from the branded merchandise. They are basically there to sell on behalf of the company and many use this business model as a way of growing and infiltrating our towns and villages. At the time of writing this book, on the Lighter-Life website, information on becoming a franchisee is readily available. It says on their website, and I quote: *'Are you thinking about starting your own business, becoming your own boss and being fully in control of when you work and what you earn? Looking for a low risk franchise that provides high returns with a low investment? You're in the right place.'*

The vast majority of people sitting in any weight loss group do not need the diet plan they are being sold.

They need help to become normal eaters.
They need help to start trusting themselves again.
They need help to begin accepting and loving themselves.
They need help to start believing they are already enough.
They need help in practicing self compassion and cutting themselves some slack.
They need help in starting to live a life which lights them up so food isn't their coping strategy anymore.
They need help in learning new ways to comfort themselves instead of walking into the kitchen at all times of day and night.
They need help in understanding the reasons why they eat like they do and what the triggers, drivers and inner programs are which make food an obsession for them.
They don't need a bloody diet plan!

And yes that also includes people who are classed as clinically obese. No matter what someone's size, their long term solution to feeling happier and confident in their skin and improving their wellbeing is found in healing their relationship with food and ultimately themselves, it's got nothing to do with focusing on losing weight as being the only solution available to them.

WHY DIETS DO NOT WORK

The diet industry is not only rooted in the failure of its customers but the system itself is the biggest failure there is. It pulls people in to wasting their time and sometimes lives striving to look like someone else in the belief that a slimmer body will make them happier and able to live a fuller life.

We know diets don't work. We know that dieting is one of the biggest causes why we become binge eaters, food obsessives, over eaters and emotional eaters with people who are dying to be thin, literally losing their lives chasing slimness. Go and take a look. There are hundreds of news reports and articles of young girls dying from taking fat burning pills, healthy sport players collapsing with heart failure after crash diets and women dying as their bodies have overheated after taking diet pills sold to boost metabolism. That's beside the countless number of women, girls, men and boys who never recover from their eating disorders, many of which started by wanting to lose a few pounds. This has got to stop.

So just incase you need anymore clarity, here are 11 reasons why diets of any kind won't ever work. Read them. Read them again and then read them some more. I need you to get this:

1. Diets focus on the food and not much else

Food is not the enemy despite what you may think through the lens of the diet industry. It's not about the food. Cake is just cake until you believe it's bad. Cheese is just cheese until you believe it has the ability to take over your mind and that's why you can't stop eating it. Chocolate is just chocolate. Bread is just bread.

Your relationship with food is far from 'balanced' and 'peaceful' right now as your head is full of food thoughts and diet thoughts as you spend every minute of the day obsessing about it all. Things that you can eat, can't eat and shouldn't eat. The rules that you have around food. The types of food, the amount of food and when you should eat the food. It's all about the goddamn food. You think food is the problem and therefore you need to address the food through diets.

Except diets completely ignore everything which makes us human....our desires, our needs, our passions, our pleasures, our emotions, our feelings and our stories, all of which are the drivers behind why we eat the way we do. It has very little to do with what we eat. So stop making food the problem. Food is just food unless you choose to believe otherwise.

2. Diets encourage you to obsess about food (especially the 'bad' food!)

When have you ever been on a diet and spent all day long obsessing about salad? Or obsessing about the taste of that fat free/carb free lunch? Or obsessing about the bowl of sugar free jelly with fat free yoghurt for desert you'll be having that evening? Let's get real, you more than likely spent all day obsessing about the cookies you can't have, the taste of chocolate which you are so desperate for but it's forbidden and the delight of having a muffin with your afternoon coffee but that's not allowed either.

No pleasure = no fun = no life.

Dieters spend most of the day thinking and obsessing about food which we spoke about with the Minnesota Starvation Experiment earlier. The more you try and restrict what you are eating and the more you try and control what you can and can't have, the more you are likely to become a food obsessed, irritated & even crazier version of yourself.

DIETS ARE THE OBSESSION, NOT THE FOOD

3. Diets are a guaranteed fast track way to an eventual binge

Imagine you've spent 2 weeks on the 'X' diet (insert the latest diet craze if you wish) and you've had your ups and downs but you've pushed through and feeling quite proud of yourself of having lived on 'X' for the last 2 weeks. I remember feeling like that when I got into week 3 of Atkins after living on meat and cream for a fortnight, both things I completely dislike. Then something happens.

Your best friend comes around with some cake. Your partner wants to take you to the cinema where there will be popcorn on offer. You have a birthday party/celebration/dinner date and there will be all kinds of food which you've banned from the house for the last 2 weeks. What happens? You convince yourself that a little taste will be ok as you nibble on a tiny piece of ciabatta from the bread basket, then you decide a little more will be fine as you finish the whole piece whilst telling yourself it's carb-free eating again now......30 minutes later you've eaten all the bread basket, you've tucked into a whole bowl of pasta, enough for the entire table and you're now half way through the richest and largest portion of chocolate fudge cake complete with ice cream. I know you've done that too!

Studies and research has shown that if you want to put weight on in the long term, go on a diet. If you want to become obsessed about food, go on a diet. If you want to reduce your self worth and self esteem, go on a diet and if you want to suffer from binge eating and food cravings, you've guessed it, go on a diet.

THE MORE YOU DIET, THE MORE YOU WILL BIN GE. IT'S A GIVEN. GUARANTEED

When you've deprived yourself from the things which actually taste nice and have elements of bringing us pleasure such as warm bread, creamy pasta and gooey chocolate cake, it's only natural that once you allow yourself to 'taste some' your mind and body go crazy....'Oh my goodness, this tastes so good. I have no idea when I'll next allow myself to have this again so I best eat some more just incase I'm not allowed it again for ages!'

4. Diets often create deprivation and restriction

As mentioned above, when we diet we significantly increase our chances of feeling deprived and at some point feeling restricted in the sense of not having freedom of choice. I would argue with anyone who claims otherwise.

Deprivation causes us to feel left out as we feel excluded when we say 'no' to the birthday cake in the office, 'no' to the popcorn in the cinema and 'no' to the glass of wine with dinner. Restriction is the same, no human being on this planet wants to feel restricted in whatever way that might be for them. Sometimes life brings us restriction which is forced upon us like not being able to move house due to money or being in a job due to circumstances but some things are easier to change and control than others. What you choose to put in your mouth is in your control and you can change that feeling of restriction immediately by changing what you eat. It really is that simple.

RESTRICTING FOOD CAUSES YOU TO RESTRICT YOUR LIFE

5. Diets focus on weight and numbers. What about wellness or happiness?

We've discussed it already and I know it's a controversial topic but weight is not reflective of health.

Who said that 'curvier' people are unhealthy? Why does slimness equal healthy? Who said that women who have lumps and bumps cannot be happy? Where is it written that states in order to be accepted within society and by our peers you must be slim and able to wear a bikini with your flat tummy and toned thighs on display? Where have these crazy ideas come from? (oh that's right, diet cult-ure!)

Some people who are incredibly slim also struggle with their self worth and relationship with food and they too can be far from happy but because their weight is in the ok range that's fine. If we truly believe the foundations on which diets are formed that it's all about what number you want and need to be, then I invite you to open your eyes and wake up! That is not the whole picture. Take these two examples:

A very slim women who smokes, doesn't exercise, is currently unemployed and depressed as she's at home all day and her husband is having an affair which she has just found out about.

A bigger women who has cellulite, a 'mummy tummy' and a wobbly bottom whose BMI is on the larger size and classed as obese, who exercises regularly, drinks lots of water, has a job which she adores and a husband who thinks the world of her, she socialises several times a week with friends and finds herself feeling very blessed and grateful for her life.

Who is the healthiest? Who is the happiest? Who is the most content? Whose state of mind would be positively affecting her wellbeing? I know these examples are somewhat extreme but it's to highlight a point which we find so difficult to see most of the time.

Dieting does not give you the key to the happy life door yet far too often that's what we buy into when we start such programs. Health is also not just physical. Do not underestimate the stress our bodies are put under when we are worrying and freaking out about what to eat and what we currently weigh. Stress hormones being released over a prolonged period will affect your health at some point in the future.

JOANNA: I'VE PUT HER THROUGH SO MUCH

....

I spent over 20 years being a chronic dieter, jumping from one crash diet to another. When I was on them I was really strict and did whatever it took to lose the weight. Exercising everyday, tracking food, somedays living on 500 calories so I could lose weight faster. When I think back I feel so sad, the things I put my poor body through is terrible.

When I turned 43 I got a chest infection which very quickly turned into pneumonia with some other complications. I was so very poorly in hospital and spent 5 days in intensive care where I very nearly lost my life and spent months recovering fully. I can't help but wonder what damage all that crash dieting and under eating has done to my long term health. It does worry me. It scares me as I can't undo it now.

6. Diets are not sustainable

I managed Atkins for 3.5 weeks and then I gave up and I gave up in style! I spent the following week compulsively overeating anything anti-Atkins. I couldn't sustain being bread free, saying no to practically everything that was being cooked at the time and always having to make excuses why I wasn't eating at lunchtime with my friends at work as the canteen didn't cater for Atkins very well.

If anything isn't sustainable and actually causes stress and difficulty, you will not stick to it as it goes against the ease and flow when something comes naturally. We all want life to be easy and we all have a right to have things as easy as possible. Eating shouldn't be any different. If food and eating causes you stress then something isn't right.

7. Diets put your life on hold, encouraging you to wait on the weight

It's inevitable that when you are trying so hard to be 'good' and stay on a diet that there are many things you don't and can't do. Spontaneous coffee mornings, birthday lunches in the office or dinner dates with the other half to name but a few. Not only do they tempt you with the 'naughty' food on offer but you potentially would also feel left out and deprived if you went (see reasons 4 and 6 again for the explanation!)

I am a huge advocate that women need to stop waiting on their weight to create and have the life they are hungry for now, so that of course includes dieting. If you are waiting until your skinny jeans fit you again and the diet works until you start saying 'yes' to the coffee mornings, dinner dates and birthday lunches, you'll find yourself in a vicious cycle of dieting, falling off, bingeing, feeling guilty and re-starting the diet again. I did that for 14 years. I don't want you to do it any longer.

8. Diets completely ignore our hungry souls + emotional hungers

I mentioned this in reason 1. The problem with diets is not only do they solely focus on food but they completely ignore something which happens to all of us, emotional hunger. You know what that is right? You fancy a biscuit with your coffee. You want popcorn at the cinema. You want some chocolate on the sofa with your partner watching a great movie and washing it down with a nice glass of red, which also happens to be my idea of a perfect evening by the way.

Food is emotional. We all have emotions and often memories and stories connected to food. Take away the food through dieting and what do you have? An emotional void that is looking for a way to be filled. Now don't get me wrong, this is slightly different to someone who is always emotionally eating as a way of pushing all the emotion inside her down and choosing to numb out. I'm referring to those moments when our desires for something pleasurable in the form of food, overrides our physical hunger and we desire something to eat which is not only normal but encouraged. Diets don't allow for this. They make us feel like a failure for giving in and make us feel guilty for not 'sticking' to the rules.

I've learnt from experience that when you embrace the fact that we all turn to food at some point for emotional support (emotional eating can perhaps never be completely 'cured') it gives you consent to eat in a different way. You eat without guilt. You eat with permission. You eat through choice. You eat feeling empowered.

You also bizarrely often don't eat because that's ok as well! I sometimes have popcorn at the cinema and sometimes not, yet when I was food-obsessed I always made a point of ordering the largest popcorn and made sure I ate every single piece including all the crumbs and un-popped kernels at the bottom, partly because I had told myself I wouldn't have popcorn next time and partly because I was feeling so guilty for ordering the popcorn in the first place that I was stuffing it in, kind of enjoying the delicious warm and sweet taste but also feeling terribly aware of the guilt bubbling up inside. Each mouthful wasn't just popcorn, I was eating the guilt too.

Imagine having a 'take it or leave it' attitude with anything you choose to eat? It's so liberating and it's available to you too.

9. Diets ignore your intuition

A woman's intuition is the most powerful force there is and I teach my clients how to reconnect to their own. When we listen to ourselves, our bodies or our gut, we are in connection with the most valuable thing which we have. Ourselves. Our inner Soul Fed Woman.

Yet diets teach us that our bodies can't be trusted and without self-trust, you are heading towards a really dysfunctional and disconnected relationship with food.

It goes like this:

Diet says: Drink water instead of eating as you probably aren't hungry

Your intuition says: No I am really hungry, I need food!!

Diet says: Have a diet soda in the afternoon to curb those sugar cravings

Your intuition says: I'd get so much satisfaction from one of those little Italian biscuits right now with a full fat latte

Diet says: You can't eat after 6pm

Intuition says: Its 6.30pm and I'm starving, feed me, I'm hungry!

Diet says: Stay away from carbs, they are bad for you

Intuition says: Some warm buttered toast is exactly when I desire for breakfast right now

10. Diets reinforce a sense of failure, low self esteem and self worth

This is particularly close to my heart as I can remember in vivid detail the feeling of failure and guilt whenever I fell off the diet wagon and I fell off them all spectacularly, many times over. Part of me would feel so worthless that I had once again broken my diet, even though another part of me was delighted that I was tucking into some pasta for dinner with full fat garlic bread. Over the years, as each diet attempt came and went, I truly started to believe it was me not being good enough, strong enough or able enough. It did nothing for my self worth, self esteem and feeling inadequate which where already at an all time low hence the reason for my need to control my food and my weight. I believed being slimmer would be the answer and suddenly I would feel freakin' amazing. Guess what though? That never happened. Each diet I embarked on helped to reinforce the beliefs I had about myself, giving me more evidence when I couldn't stick to the rules.

If you feel rubbish about yourself, if you don't think you are good enough, able enough or worthy enough, I encourage you to stop dieting and stop controlling your food. This is adding to the problem. Incidentally some studies have shown a connection between low self esteem and feelings of inadequacy being linked noticeably to binge eating. Everything is connected.

11. Diets ignore our subconscious emotional attachment to food

We all have a food or a meal which makes us smile when we think about it or makes our mouth water when we imagine sitting down to it. These foods are almost always associated and connected to happy times and lovely memories, often from childhood. This subconscious programming and emotional attachment to certain foods make it impossible to give them up as we have stories, memories and feelings associated with them.

We'll be discussing emotional eating further on in the book but notice how often you seek to change your emotions through food. We choose food to pick us up. We choose food to make us feel safe. We choose food to make us feel happy. In fact we choose food to make us feel better in so many ways. It could be seen that food becomes our comfort blanket and shield of protection. So when these foods are not allowed on our diet and our emotional state is not even considered, is it any wonder that many of us feel even more stressed and upset? We find ourselves dieting and all of our favourite comfort foods are now banned! So there you are having a stressful day, all you want is a piece of cake which obviously isn't allowed so you become even more irritated, fed up and stressed leaving you with an emptiness you desperately want to fill. And the easiest way? Eat the cake regardless, break the diet rules and the cycle continues.

STEP TWO:
BODY NEUTRALITY
IN A WORLD OF BODY
PERFECTION

The Media + Body Image

Shame is the most powerful master emotion. It's the fear that we're not good enough - Brene Brown

Imagine a woman who is a 'plus size' (I loath that term but will use it to demonstrate the point.) She feels embarrassed with her body as she walks down the street as, we have discussed, we live in a fat phobic society and being 'fat' is seen as socially unacceptable. She orders some food in a cafe and once again feels judged with the sandwich on her plate as people can see her food choices and, heaven forbid, she didn't order a salad! Then she goes clothes shopping and can't squeeze herself into the unrealistic clothing sizes available in many of the high street stores and as she catches a glimpse of herself in the changing room mirrors, she feels deeply ashamed of how she looks. Society has been telling her for as long as she can remember that her body is not acceptable and is wrong. That she is not acceptable and is wrong. She starts thinking about dieting again, perhaps sees one of the cleverly created marketing campaigns in the magazine she's reading and as she compares her body to the photo starring up at her, she feels so ashamed of who she is.

This happens to women across the globe on a daily basis.

Embarrassment and shame are present in almost all women who struggle with food and their bodies. To clarify, embarrassment is something which is known or revealed to others and is the response to something which may be morally neutral, yet socially unacceptable with public humiliation sometimes being involved. Shame, on the other hand, is known only to us and is the response to something which we believe is morally wrong. Public humiliation is not necessarily involved.

So where does shame and embarrassment really come from? Why would any of us feel embarrassed with our bodies and ashamed of how we look?

Let's enter the media world.

We are all typically subjected to a huge amount of influence from the media concerning body size, which tends to have the widespread effect of making us dissatisfied with our own bodies. This relentless negativity is very bad for our mental health and how we feel about ourselves. Social media and the twisted body images it produces is failing women both young and old by turning them into self critical food obsessed individuals. Our quest for perfectionism doesn't stop with what we are eating by tracking, monitoring and measuring the macros and micros for the entire week, it's also influencing how we feel about our bodies.

You only need to take a look at social media and even mainstream publications to see how deeply ingrained body obsession has become within our culture and society. People, and I'm talking particularly women, are frequently praised for their weight loss. They are admired for losing weight. Yet they are openly criticised and judged for gaining weight, wearing unflattering clothes or being seen in public without make up!

Striving for perfectionism in how we eat is one thing, but chasing a perfect appearance is something else, after all having the "perfect body" is what any dieter wants. So what's your vision of the perfect body? What aspects of your body do you believe aren't perfect and you want to change or fix them? Where has that belief come from that your body isn't perfect? And why is that even important to you in the first place?

I want to invite you to start questioning the social ideal of the female body. I cannot stress this enough. That image of perfection that women compare themselves to is not healthy, it is not perfect and it's often not even real thanks to editing software like photoshop and the copious number of filters available on smartphones. Yet we hang on to that image, making it very real. We fantasise and dream about becoming that image one day when we succeed at eating perfectly and sticking to our plan. Personally, for my 5 year old daughter's sake, I want to see all edited, airbrushed and altered images in mainstream publications marked as such, like a disclaimer, telling the reader that what they are looking at is fake, or better still, not altering the images at all!

YOU WILL NEVER BE LIKE THE WOMAN IN THE MAGAZINE. EVEN SHE DOESN'T LOOK LIKE THE WOMAN IN THE MAGAZINE!

I want to be honest with you, being a perfectionist in this area of your life does not serve you, it just reinforces negative feelings towards who you are and your body and leaves you constantly comparing yourself to others.

This may surprise you to learn but over the years I've worked with several fitness models and you'd be forgiven for wondering why on earth they would need my help. After all they have the "perfect body" and must have this sorted when it comes to eating and body image, haven't they? I can tell you first hand that their carefully curated instagram feed are often not reflective of the life they are living. Yes they have abs and yes they have society's perception of the 'perfect' female body, however, they are crying in to their chicken and broccoli which they have prepared for the entire week as that's the level of restriction and obsession they need in order to look that way whilst frequently suffering from anxiety and fear of gaining weight. That's no way to live. Can you imagine how that would affect your mental health, eating the same meal pretty much every single day, week after week after week? Can you imagine how much emotional stress that would also cause? Having to turn down anything in the form of an invitation because of their incredibly strict way of eating?

One of my clients who was a bikini model told me that she realised her food obsession had got out of hand when she started taking a small set of scales wherever she went so she could weigh her food when ordering in restaurants. I kid you not. And that is just the tip of the iceberg.

EXERCISE: DROP THE PERFECTIONISM

If you choose to let some of your perfectionism go regarding how you eat and what your body looks like, how would that affect your daily life?

How could you start embracing your imperfections?

What imperfections are you open to learning how to accept?

MEDIA EXPOSURE + BODY IMAGE IDEALS

Every week all over the world, millions of publications are released in which 'perfect' women are shown laughing, having fun and dressed in beautiful clothes with their Hollywood smiles. It's really hard not to indirectly compare ourselves to everything we see and are exposed to as we are surrounded by adverts, billboards, instagram feeds, magazines & tv shows in which 'perfection' is portrayed in a way which the majority of us will never look like.

Here are some figures which might leave you wide eyed and opened mouthed. Some lifestyle and fashion magazines contain as much as 85% adverts, with around 85% of beauty magazine content being dedicated to making you feel imperfect and inadequate and in a quick survey 70% of women reported feeling guilty, depressed or ashamed within 3 minutes of reading a fashion magazine. And it isn't just the amount of products being advertised, it's how the truth is being manipulated. Several years ago H&M admitted to using computer generated body images in their advertising, so the bodies wearing their clothes weren't even real, they were fictitious and fake, yet we as the customers didn't know that. What's more is the average age of readers for many higher end fashion magazines is around 40, yet you'll be hard pushed to find many 40 year old models throughout an entire publication which is not only denying human biology but also creating a negative body image for the typical reader by promoting an illusion which destroys her self esteem.

Speaking of fashion models, the average age of one is 21

years old, she weighs 25% less than the average women and is 7 inches or 17 cm taller so statistically many fall into the underweight range of body to height ratio if BMI is to be believed (I'm not saying that models are unhealthy, I'm merely saying that statistically they are an exception to most of us.) Yet how often have you seen an image of a model and felt envious of her body and told yourself you can look like her if you tried hard enough? I did it all the bloody time without ever fully realising how my body could never ever look like her body no matter how hard I tried or whether I copied her exact eating plan and exercise regime.

This desire to look like someone else, someone who is on a pedestal when it comes to beauty and perfection can be a catalyst for some significant mental health issues. According to the current statistics from the organisation BEAT, the UK's Eating Disorder Charity, there are approximately 1.25 million people in the UK who have an eating disorder, 89% of which are female and there are many more who are not yet diagnosed. Figures seen by The Guardian show that the number of admissions to hospital of patients with potentially life-threatening eating disorders has almost doubled since 2011 and this latest data shows admissions are the highest they have been in at least a decade.

There has been a surge in the number of teenage girls and women in their early 20s behind this dramatic rise but also, for the first time, more teenage boys than ever before. This confirms what we already know that eating disorders are on the increase and must be increasing for a reason.

Although they typically develop during adolescence, a time when most girls start their first diets, it isn't uncommon for eating disorders to develop at any time in life. Children as young as 6 years old with anorexia have been identified and although there is no single cause for eating disorders developing, we do know that body insecurities and dieting are major contributors to what can be years of having severe and debilitating effects on the sufferers and their families.

GIRLS DON'T SIMPLY DECIDE TO HATE THEIR BODIES. WE TEACH THEM TO HATE THEIR BODIES.

In 2017 a survey was carried out for the Dove Global Girls Beauty and Confidence Report. Of the 5,165 girls aged 10 to 17 in 14 countries who were surveyed, it was found that 61% of girls in the UK had low body esteem (ie they didn't like their bodies). The co-author Phillippa Diedrichs, associate professor from the Centre for Appearance Research, University of the West of England, said: "These findings indicate that, despite valiant efforts, body image remains an issue for girls not only in the UK, but globally, too. We still have an enormous amount of work to do in helping girls develop the resilience they need to overcome the impact of beauty and appearance pressures. We also need to change the social and cultural environment directly so that girls are not judged on their looks and are not held back from getting a seat at whatever table they want, be it in the boardroom, or in parliament, because of body image concerns."

Nine out of 10 girls in the UK with low body esteem told the researchers they stopped themselves from eating or otherwise put their health at risk and said they avoided seeing friends and family or trying out for a team or club and close to 25% cared more about their appearance than their physical health. Placing such an importance on appearance over physical health is coming from somewhere and you have to question whether media influencers and celebrities are playing a significant role in having an effect on these young women. Now I know that as grown women we may not be as swayed towards celebrities as younger women, but when it comes to weight loss, the celebrity dieter is everyone's inspiration.

I'll be the first to admit, I was a magazine junkie when I was food and weight obsessed, often buying them based on the front cover which claimed would help me 'Drop 10lbs for Summer' or 'Learn The Latest Weight Loss Craze Which Works' or 'How to Eat Chocolate and Still Lose Weight Fast'. They were always a load of shit which never delivered on their empty promises but I would buy them anyway and then spend the rest of the week feeling more insecure about my body. Just because we are surrounded by this environmental toxicity doesn't mean you have to bring it into your home, into your sacred space or into your life. It's your choice. If you have any subscriptions to these kind of lifestyle magazines and becoming body confident, happy in your skin and ending your roller-coaster relationship with food is important to you, then please cancel your subscriptions. Stop buying them and stop buying in to them. I personally felt lighter no longer reading that stuff and haven't picked one up in over a decade.

Now some of those magazines I bought because of the 'before' and 'after' picture of some celebrity or other. Those images are often the final product of a very intricate and I think deceitful marketing plan. I'm not a huge fan of the celebrity world, not any more. Not like I used to be. Yet there is something about celebrity dieters which fascinates me at the same time as making me feel very sad and angry.

We've all seen and witnessed the celebrity yo-yo dieter. You can probably think of several right away. One minute they are pictured in a very 'unflattering' bikini on the beach in Spain whilst jumping around in a very public place and in a very unnatural way or having a training session outside in the park wearing a crop top and hot pants in the middle of winter! The next moment, they are featured in the magazines, papers and on TV promoting their weight loss video just in time for Christmas telling the audience that those unflattering photos from earlier on in the year devastated them so much that they decided to do something about it. There are copious celebrities whom I could mention right now and I'm sure you can think of several, but honestly the names are irrelevant.

When I was at the peak of my dysfunctional relationship with food and my body, I bought in to the celebrity dieting craze. Seeing a celebrity in a mainstream magazine talking about her two dress size weight loss would always be enough for me to buy their DVDs, book or their eating and exercise plans. I was a marketers dream! I had no idea at the time that the celebrity dieters are part of a very clever orchestrated marketing ploy. Allow me to elaborate.

In this celebrity obsessed world, particularly for the women, their bodies are often not their own for they are used first and foremost as a commodity which can be monetised. A pawn for promoting themselves and selling their stuff, often making them and their agents more money and increasing their PR opportunities.

You know those photos we see splashed throughout the tabloids and in the magazines of the "out-of-shape" celebrity jumping up and down on the beach? They aren't as real as they appear for they are frequently staged. The celebrity works in collaboration with a photographer who 'accidentally' captures these unflattering shots of her, selling them to the tabloids and the magazines, making themselves and the celebrity some money. I have been told, depending on who the celebrity may be, these photos can exchange hands for tens of thousands of pounds.

Then what? The celebrity is then approached to either create and develop a weight loss program off the back of these unflattering photos or gets stuck into creating the already signed DVD contract. The photos were just part of the marketing campaign running in the background to fuel media and public interest in her weight loss journey.

Fast forward a few months, particularly around mid to late November, their DVD launches showcasing their dramatic weight loss simply by following the exercise program which you can now also do in the comfort of your own home for just £10.99!

Shockingly and sadly, unbeknown to the slim hungry consumers, the celebrities can be under so much pressure to drop their weight and often do so very quickly in an unsafe way, in order for their weight loss goals to be achieved for which their contracts and their money depend upon. Starvation diets and exercising several times a day is not uncommon for these women to get their body DVD cover ready.

I know this sounds very cynical but how often have you seen within the space of the following 12 months the same celebrity once again splashed throughout the tabloids and the magazines in yet another bikini shot deemed as unflattering? However, this time the headlines are critical and judgemental commenting on her unprecedented weight gain. How many times have you seen interviews of celebrities on the verge of tears talking about how their weight has gone up and how uncomfortable they feel but they have now decided to finally take back their control? Then what? DVD number two! The wheels of the next PR campaign turn once more propelling said celebrity onto the couches of TV shows whilst exploiting the commodity of her body, and before long the DVD is on the shelves, generating thousands of pounds in revenue as young and not so young women look up to their idol, who has managed to lose the weight once again. It's painful to witness particularly when you know what's really going on behind-the-scenes. They are simply a piece in this game, where the only commodity of value is their body and what it looks like, not their intellect, not their talents, not their gifts, just the size of their thighs, how wobbly their tummy is and how big their backside appears.

I'm telling you this as it's time that you as the consumer fully understand, appreciate and acknowledge the bullshit that goes into these so-called stories. These women are being exploited for their bodies and how they look so that 'normal' woman feel inadequate and spend the money on their products in the hope that they too can get a six pack by working out for 10 minutes a day. I used to buy into this as well. Now I'm not saying at all that these women are doing anything against their will, however, by partaking in it they open themselves up to getting trapped in the dieting/weight gain cycle which no doubt is the foundation for creating dysfunctional eating and a screwed up image of themselves in the process. They haven't got their bodies by the DVD that they are trying to sell you. They haven't dropped two dress sizes easily and effortlessly by just following their simple eating plan which you can now find in their weight-loss book. They look like they do on the DVD cover because they haven't eaten much in the days and weeks leading up to the photoshoot, feeling light headed and dizzy through starvation whilst they stand there smiling in their bikinis and tensing their stomach muscles. Their entire lives now revolve around food, calories, exercise and weight maintenance that this can be the start of an incredibly slippery slope towards food dysfunction and body image anxiety.

I find celebrity endorsed weight loss products incredibly infuriating not to mention ridiculously irresponsible. Think about how many vulnerable people and young girls who see their idols promoting 'appetite suppressant lollipops' or 'flat tummy teas' and believe that being slimmer is all they can offer the world. As a woman and a mother to a daughter, it just goes to show how deeply ingrained and accepted dieting is that these women don't see what they are doing is morally irresponsible. I'm not painting the entire celebrity world as being like this, there are equally some powerhouse women standing up for body positivity and female empowerment, but those who aren't definitely add to the problem which many of us are trying to fight.

Whilst we are on the subject, how many male celebrity dieters can you think of? My point exactly. There are a significantly larger number of female celebrities who are famous because they are yo-yo dieters, valued and seen in magazines based on weight loss or weight gain. Male celebrities, on the other hand, are frequently reported on for their achievements and acknowledged for their talents, it's never about their bodies or what they are wearing. Check in any daily newspaper and you'll see what I'm talking about. Language used for describing a woman almost always focuses on her clothes, body and appearance whilst the language used for describing a man almost always focuses on his successes, achievements and strengths. What's more we see this inequality on gender specific clothing with girl's t-shirts commonly printed with slogans such as 'Future Trophy Wife,' 'I'm too pretty to do my homework' and 'I look fabulous' whilst the boy's equivalent says 'Future Scientist,' 'Brave and Strong' and 'Future Man of Steel'. In fact here in the UK one supermarket was slammed for its blatant sexist children's clothing when they produced two identical t-shirts with two very different messages. The boy's one said 'Little Man, Big Ideas' and the girl's one said 'Little Girl, Big Smiles'. As a parent to both a son and a daughter this isn't ok. What do you think? If you had a daughter and the only thing that she was encouraged to value was her appearance, translated as the size and shape of her body which will inevitably fluctuate throughout her life, would that not make you incredibly upset and angry?

EXERCISE: GO ON A DETOX (OF THE MEDIA KIND!)

....

How many people or things do you surround yourself with who make you feel inadequate in terms of how you look? How many people do you compare yourself to? How many people make you feel insecure and uncomfortable in your own body? Possibly way too many if you are honest.

Take a step back from your environmental influences by unfollowing people/companies/brands and unsubscribing from email lists and magazines. Start choosing what and who you wish to be surrounded by.

BODY DIVERSITY AND SOCIAL COMPARISON

Watch any tv program or movie, flick open a magazine (although I've just encouraged you to ditch the lifestyle ones as they are full of screwed perceptions of female bodies) or even see a billboard or an advertisement in a shop and find someone who has the same body as you with cellulite, perhaps a mummy tummy and noticeable lumps and bumps.

The chances are you won't and this brings us on to this topic.....body diversity and social comparison.

KATE: I DON'T STARVE MYSELF ANYMORE

....

When I was thinner I would get recognition and admiration from people saying how great I looked and to keep up the good work. Despite feeling weak, dizzy and food obsessed, I was constantly receiving cultural reinforcement that thin was better. Today I no longer try and live up to the crazy beauty ideals of how my body is supposed to look. I don't starve myself anymore. I focus on what I do with my life rather than the size of my waist.

We all compare ourselves to others but why do we do that? Well the answer is actually quite simple. As we grow up we need a way of figuring out how we fit into the world and we do that by comparison. We start to look around to see where and how we fit in by answering subconscious questions such as am I clever, am I a gifted artist, am I good at sport, am I shy/nervous/confident? This is also applicable for our body too as we naturally compare ours to everyone else's bodies highlighting whether we are tall, slim, short or fatter than others.

We do this because there is no universal meter stick for our talents, characteristics or abilities. Every single one of us will, at some time, compare but how we feel about that comparison is dependent on who is around us and also on our level of self-esteem. When I was at school I was terrible at cross country running (and I mean terrible....think the last out of 60 kids!) Now if at the time there had only been a few children who were faster than I was, I might have been ok with that. If I had only ever run on my own around that muddy field, I may have believed that I was great at cross country running as I couldn't have gone into comparison mode but when it appears that everyone around me was better than I was, it made me feel inadequate and rubbish at running, which resulted in my avoiding ever running again until I was in my 20s for this reason!

The same applies to our perceptions of our bodies due to lack of body diversity and inclusion. If the only bodies you are surrounded by are cellulite free Victoria's Secret models, fitness fanatics with six packs on your facebook and instagram feed and 5ft 11+ models and actresses on the tv and movie screens, is it any wonder that the majority of women feel inadequate about their physical appearances?

Lack of body diversity is a major issue and I believe a significant contributor to the rise of eating disorders within our fat phobic society. It's a topic which many people, groups and organisations are tirelessly campaigning about, but the reality is that the dialogue around this subject is exhausting as so many people, brands and establishments don't want to listen. I've known campaigners who have been silenced and bullied by global sport brands for speaking up on social media and calling them out on their lack of diversity and inclusion within their marketing. Yet this is the truth. Bodies do come in all shapes and sizes yet women who are not a size 8-10 are rarely ever included in retail sport brands. Runners, swimmers, cyclists, netball players, hockey players and footballers come in every size and shape imaginable so why do we only ever see tall, slim, athletically built models wearing the brands….? And it isn't just sport brands, it's pretty much all mainstream, high street chains. Look at the mannequins in windows, the posters on display and any advertising material in magazines, they are not representational of the majority of women out there.

It's 2018 and yet we are still having these conversations!

I can remember being in tears in fitting rooms trying to squeeze my cellulite dimpled wobbly thighs into jeans which were 'supposed' to fit me based on the label size yet so often didn't even come past my knees. I'm sure you've experienced the craziness of clothes sizes too. Take a size 14 from 10 different stores and they will all be slightly different in dimensions, some more than others so no wonder we become so despondent when the clothes don't fit, creating all kinds of stories in our minds about overnight weight gain and needing to diet once more. Yet it's not you. It's them! I was shocked to discover that some chains and designers even started adding extra material to their clothes without changing the sizes on the labels as they noticed sales go up when the dress sizes come down. This was the start of what has since been termed vanity sizing for it has been shown that women generally feel better about themselves when they fit into smaller than expected sizes. Not only does this highlight another example of how companies are hacking the psychology of their buyers based on their body insecurities but it also demonstrates how we are so deeply concerned about our body size. We need that reassurance so much that we are thin that our emotional reaction overpowers logic when it comes to consumer buyer behaviour.

Speaking of clothes sizes, did you know that prior to the 1940s, most women's clothing was made-to-measure so there was really no need for standardised sizing? So when consumer buyer behaviour changed and ready-made clothing hit the high streets, everything changed with it. Sizes were introduced by attempting to quantify the average American female body and it was the government which introduced the numbers and who decided what the dimensions of each size was, and guess what? They used men's chest measurements as their model even though women's bust sizes are, of course, a lot more variable.

Which leads me to ask you how would you feel if all the mannequins in clothes shops or models on catwalks and in magazines were representative of the 'average' women which is a size 16 in the UK or 12-14 in the USA? How would you feel if your body size and shape regularly appeared within mainstream media such as adverts and tv shows? How would you feel if clothing companies and high street stores produced clothes without a need for a 'plus size' line? Simply all clothes, in all sizes, all together, for all women with no need to separate them!

It would be amazing wouldn't it?

When it comes to body shapes, there is no normal. Everyone's body is different. Curves are beautiful, but so are no curves. Being bigger is beautiful, but so is being smaller. We all need to stand together on this one and start realising that no woman is the same, rather than holding one particular body as the most desirable one. Without us continuing to talk about this and calling brands out, nothing will change and the patriarchal systems which lead us here in the first place will continue unless we deliberately start dismantling them and choosing to no longer play the game. I have a 5 year old daughter who I am already ferociously protecting from the society she is growing up in saying her body will not be included and accepted as being 'normal' unless she is a size 10 and looks a certain way.

Open your eyes gorgeous. It's all around you. Start noticing the lack of body diversity within every part of our culture and society as once you notice it, you'll start to see how this truly has influenced the way you view your body and compare yourself, fuelled your constant desire to lose weight and led you to being food obsessed and struggling with binge eating and overeating.

This isn't your fault but it's your responsibility to start taking your power back with it.

REDEFINING BEAUTY

It isn't possible to fully make peace with your body without challenging your beliefs around beauty and body image.

I want you to think about what beauty is for you? Who would you say is beautiful in your eyes? Does their size and body shape influence your choice or are you choosing someone who radiates that special something irrelevant of their size and shape or what the label says in their clothes?

It might be difficult to admit this to yourself but you have fear around different body types especially feeling scared of putting on weight and so you diet to lose weight as you don't want to get fat. We have become so influenced that some body types are seen as bad which we must stay away from i.e. 'fat' and some body types are good which we must strive towards i.e. 'slim'. I remember asking my community what perceptions they had of thinner people compared to fatter people and it was clear from their responses that there is an unspoken assumption that slim people are somehow happier, healthier, more successful, more desirable, more active and more loveable than fat people. Would you agree?

These sociological factors at play here cannot be ignored - we are surrounded by them, influenced by them, brainwashed and conditioned by them.

So let's take a closer look.

Our body image is formed at an early age and is based on

all the external messages which we are being given from the world in which we live. All these messages, combined with our immediate surroundings of family and friends, can either help us to develop a positive and healthy body image or it can create the opposite.

Family is our earliest influence when it comes to body image so have a think about your family dynamic when it came to bodies. What did your family believe? What messages were you given about body types? Did you have parents who themselves had distorted body image issues such as a dieting mum or a food obsessed dad? Sometimes comments can be made about our bodies when we are growing up and even though they may not have been meant maliciously or they weren't said to be hurtful, they can impact our perception of ourselves. If you were teased about your nose, your height or your weight, this can lay the foundations for a shaky body image as you grow older.

AMANDA: MY SLIMMER TWIN

....

I grew up with my non-identical twin sister. Although we are non identical we do look ridiculously alike. I remember from such a young age how people would talk about her as being the prettier one. She had shinier hair, a straighter nose and when we got older she was slimmer too. I had this constant reminder, all day every day, of what it would be like to be slimmer, more accepted and more desirable as she was the mirror image of a slimmer me.

School and our social circle becomes a very influential time as we get older. Our family influence starts to take a back seat and instead our peers and friends at school start to influence us. Around this time we also start to go through puberty, which can be a really unsettling time for many particularly as our bodies start to change shape and size and it can be during these influential times when comments or suggestions made by others can really impact how we view ourselves and our bodies. I was a late developer and flat chested at school and it was often the centre of many a classroom and playground joke which became a catalyst for my own 14 year body and weight obsession. How might your body image have been influenced when you were at school?

GEMMA: HUMILIATED AT SCHOOL

....

When I was about 13 or 14 I remember having a crush on some- one at school. I thought he was really cute and it was the first time I had feeling towards a boy. I'd always been a little chubbier than my friends but I don't remember ever being conscious of it or it bothering me until this incident. I remember like this happened yesterday. We were in the school hall for some kind of assembly and I was about to sit next to him when he said I couldn't as I was too fat and a few of the other kids giggled......I remember feeling so humiliated, embarrassed, ashamed and hurt. I carried that with me for decades, never wanting to be the 'fat one' and I know that affected how I felt about my body for years and why food became a constant battle.

And it doesn't stop there. Think about toys you played with and the types of cartoons and films you were exposed to. Barbie has been criticised for her unrealistic proportions as have Disney princesses from all of the movies.......it's an in- teresting point though isn't it? When children are lead to be- lieve this is what a princess looks like and Barbie becomes an accepted physical representation of a woman, you can under- stand how some of those early messages can pave the way for body insecurity forming in later life.

EXERCISE: YOUR BODY IMAGE

....

Where might some of your body insecurities have come from? Think about comments made to you, things which embarrassed you and any incidents which made you feel humiliated. Write them all down.

BODY NEUTRALITY - NOT BODY LOVE

As you step away from diets and you allow your own body wisdom to reawaken whilst gently leaning into trusting what you hear, you will realise how important it is for you to take steps towards self approval. No amount of dieting, trying to be 'good' with food or losing weight will ever give you the approval that you are already enough. That must come from you. Always. The more we fight our so called imperfections, our wobbly tummies, our undefined arms and our cellulite covered thighs, the more obsessed we become on trying to diet and the more hatred we start to manifest towards ourselves. We are literally feeding this cycle all the time. You may have heard people talk about body acceptance but how on earth can we accept something which we judge so much and which we have so much emotion attached to? The truth of the matter is that we have to find a way as no one built a truly rewarding relationship with anyone, let alone themselves, founded on hate and disgust.

YOU CAN'T LOVE YOUR BODY OR YOURSELF FULLY IF YOU KEEP WISHING IT IS SOMETHING DIFFERENT.

You've probably heard of the body positive movement and the notion of practicing body love, yet I'm guessing they somehow feel a little off for you? If so, I hear you as they do for me too. The thought of loving ourselves when we can't even stand to look at our own reflections without beating ourselves up seems impossible. I think it's very misleading in a society which is constantly telling us and teaching us that we aren't good enough, to expect women to suddenly be able to turn 180 and start embracing body love when they've been beating themselves up for decades whilst diet culture shouts even louder that slimness is more desirable. I know that body acceptance, let alone body love, is a huge challenge for many women who believe deep down that losing weight is the only solution to liking themselves. I get it. That's what I believed too. Yet when we are constantly coming from a place of comparing our body to everyone else's, coming from a place of hating and disliking our bodies and therefore ourselves, our lack of body acceptance is feeding the fire. Feeding the desperation. Feeding the obsession of chasing the illusive dream of being slim. By the way, please be very mindful of movements, brands and individuals who talk about body positivity, body acceptance and body love whilst still equating slimness to being healthy and better for us. Body positivity, body acceptance and body love should never be seen in the same conversation as 'let me show you how to love and accept yourself whilst losing the weight' and if it is, then someone is completely missing the entire point of this work and I encourage you to walk away from them!

Focusing on body love as being the final destination is not only incredibly challenging when we are coming from a place of judgement but it's also likely to take a lot of hard and challenging work to override how we really feel, thanks to all of the topics which we've already been discussing.

There is, however, an easier or more aligned way. One of the things which I encourage my clients to begin practicing is body neutrality not body love. Let me explain.

As you begin following the steps in this book, your relationship with food will begin to change and at some point, you can expect to reach a place of food neutrality, meaning food is just food. Chocolate is just chocolate. An apple is just an apple. You give no meaning to it as you no longer pass judgement on what or how you are eating. It is from a place of food neutrality where food obsession, binge eating and emotional eating also begin to disappear as you have removed emotional attachment from food choice. The same is true with your body. Getting to a place where your body is simply a vessel in which you live, albeit a very sophisticated and incredible one, is when weight obsession and body insecurities also begin to vanish.

Very few women walk around loving their arms, adoring their thighs and fully accepting their stretch marks and mummy tummies, it's not realistic in a world which is forever bombarding us with the messages of how we should be looking. I don't look at any of my body parts and feel love for them. I appreciate my body as a whole as it's where I live, but I don't love any of the parts yet nor do I detest them as I have done in the past. My body isn't me. I'm me. My body is the vehicle in which I get to experience life in whatever way I choose.

So what if you could start practicing body neutrality where you have no opinion either way of your body? Your stomach isn't good or bad. Your stretch marks are neither lovely nor hideous and your cellulite is neither wonderful or disgusting. It's all neutral. It simply is what it is. I believe it is completely possible to fully appreciate, look after and be grateful for your body for what she has done for you and what she allows you to do without ever getting to a place of fully loving your body parts. When we take judgement out, it allows us to view ourselves from a place of neutrality which eventually often leads to acceptance.

In an ideal world it would be incredible if you could move away from body insecurities straight to body acceptance, but for most people that is a journey which can take a little bit of time, so whilst you are doing that, I'm inviting you to change your perception. Instead of hating on her, instead of prodding her in the mirror every time you get undressed and instead of poking her through your clothes, what if you could start reminding yourself that this is where you are living right now regardless of what you think about her and you have two choices? Either carry on the negative, critical and judgemental self talk and pull yourself into a deep hole of feeling horrible (which ironically is when you might turn to food as you feel so fed up and low that you want to eat your way out of it!) or change your perception by learning to switch off the inner dialogue of your thoughts, bringing yourself back to neutrality.

LOOK AT WHY YOU CAN'T ACCEPT YOUR BODY. RECOGNISE THIS ISN'T YOUR FAULT. IT COMES FROM A SOCIETY WITH DEEP SYSTEMATIC BIAS TOWARDS CERTAIN BODY TYPES

The thoughts you have about your body aren't you. Not the real you. Not your soul fed woman for she doesn't judge herself. She observes, witnesses and pays attention but doesn't judge, criticise, punish or hate on herself. She recognises why we feels the way she does. Learning to be neutral about your imperfections really is an incredible foundation to lay down but one which most of us ignore or bypass as for years we've conditionally accepted our bodies based on her weight or her size. When our sense of self-acceptance and self-worth is tied to our weight, we start loving ourselves more when we slim down but the minute the weight goes back on again, which it will as diets don't work, we love ourselves much less. This is no way to live nor is it a strategy which will ever lead to long term happiness.

As I said, loving our bodies need not be the desired destination as I honestly don't believe you have to love your body completely to significantly improve your body confidence. So how about reframing the destination? What if you could try and be your own best friend from now? If best friend is a step too far, then start with friend. How would you choose to speak to yourself? How would you choose to see yourself? What advice would you offer when you are feeling inadequate, fed up and in a bit of a mood?

Body neutrality is not about throwing in the towel by the way. It is not about saying to yourself, 'oh sod it I might as well just eat myself into oblivion!' It's not about no longer caring. It's not about giving up on yourself. It's actually the complete opposite. I often liken body neutrality to waving a metaphorical white flag for it's about you making a decision to finally stop the fight. The fight with your body. The fight with food. The fight with yourself. The fight with the entire topic.

Body neutrality is about truly stepping into that place of making yourself the centre of your world whilst practising self compassion, sprinkling in some self kindness with some metaphorical and emotional hugs and choosing to live your life and look after yourself which show you are worthy and deserving of it all. Neutrality frequently leads to acceptance of our bodies, which overtime helps us to take care of our bodies better. I know that acceptance can be challenging, after all we live in a world which tells us we shouldn't accept, yet speaking from experience, until anyone accepts themselves, they will continue to chase weight loss as the solution to feeling better about themselves as diet culture sells the idea that slimness equals happiness which simply isn't true.

START WITH BODY NEUTRALITY AND SEE WHERE YOU GO FROM THERE.

Part of the food freedom process for many, if not most

women, is eventually accepting a body which is bigger than the goal they may have spent decades working towards and that can trigger something similar to a grief process. I encourage you to be kind with yourself as you explore this topic and if you do feel sad, angry, upset or fed up then use the free resources which come with this book, especially tapping or EFT.

Special extra note for mums:

Calling all mamas! Many reports and studies have shown a connection between parents' attitude towards dieting and children's behaviour and I'm sure that this won't surprise you but most children, even as young as five, have the same beliefs about food as their parents. Please be mindful of how you talk about yourself in front of your children, even when you don't think they can hear. They are learning through example. This isn't to reprimand you and make your feel terrible, God knows how challenging being a parent is already, it's to gently remind you that if you want your children to grow up feeling confident and happy in their own skin, it starts with you working on getting to that place for yourself. Don't pull yourself down in front of them. Don't criticise your body or theirs, ever. Focus on the incredible job your body and their bodies do every day to help you have fun and smile. One way you can do this is to talk about bodies as being strong, healthy and happy. Avoid discussing or referencing the size of body parts, the same way that you don't compare who has bigger or smaller feet as it's not important, relevant or necessary.

And all you mama bears out there, it's totally ok to challenge others who may innocently reference your child's body. You are leading the way of helping others shift their perception whilst leading by example as your children grow up. I remember once speaking up when a family friend prodded my 2 year old daughter's tummy whilst she was eating an ice-cream and said 'look at that big fat tummy, is that ice cream tasty??' I know it wasn't meant maliciously but it's not ok to pass comment on other people's bodies, so speak up and say something. It's comments like that one which can stay with people for decades and become the catalyst for food dysfunction and weight obsession.

STEP THREE:
FEELINGS NEED TO BE
FELT, NOT FED

Emotional Eating + Binging

The biggest damage with emotional eating and binging is not the act itself. It's holding onto the guilt and shame of what you've done for days.

I'm hoping by now you've realised that your desire to lose weight or maintain weight through the habit of dieting, fulled by society's perception of what you think you should look like, has created this self destructive and dysfunctional relationship with food and yourself, one of which manifests itself in the form of emotional eating and/or binge eating. Now before we proceed I want to make it super clear that neither emotional eating or binging are fundamentally wrong, it's simply a coping strategy or a behavioural response to life which many of us end up adopting for whatever reason and to be fair I don't think it's entirely possible to get rid of emotional eating completely, nor in fact should any of us try to.

There will always be a part of emotional eating when it comes to food. That is normal. We eat birthday cake to join in with the celebration and we have a biscuit with our coffee whilst catching up with a best friend. These are still moments of eating emotionally as we may not be physically hunger at the time but we are driven by our emotions to eat regardless. However, the difference being that those moments bring with them no guilt or shame, they are free from emotional attachment. So to make the clear distinction of what I'm talking about, it's when we feel out of control in the process and emotionally attached to what we are doing or what we did.

Although emotional eating and binging are often talked about as separate issues, I'd argue otherwise and for the sake of our conversation I'm putting them together. It is uncommon to ever have one without the other and as you'll see, their causes and characteristics also overlap. What I have witnessed, personally and professionally, is an emotional eater will often binge once she starts and, likewise, a binge eater is often an emotional eater with emotional eating tending to precede a binge, a bit like this.

1. You eat a biscuit as you are feeling fed up.

2. Then you feel guilty for eating a biscuit as you are trying to be 'good'

3. You think to yourself 'what the hell, I might as well keep eating the biscuits'

4. You find yourself binge eating the biscuits, one after another until they've all gone or you feel sick.

5. You then continue to beat yourself up for being so weak willed and tell yourself you'll be good again tomorrow.

I remember living in this cycle for the entire duration of my dysfunctional relationship with food and I know that this cycle is all too familiar with you too as we've all been there, having a stressful day at work and desperately needing chocolate. Or a stressful afternoon with the children and needing biscuits. Or an uncomfortable situation with family or friends and needing junk food.

Sometimes it can be pretty much impossible to stop those urges to go crazy with food, especially when there has been something to trigger that urge. I have to say that in all the years of working with women, some of the most common emotional triggers for emotional eating and binging are feeling out of control, anxiety and overwhelm, all of which create a stress response within the body. Turning to food in those moments is really common and yet, despite what you think, it has nothing to do with lack of willpower or not being strong enough to resist the urges. It does, however, have everything to do with these reasons:

1. Sugar Cravings

Whenever we are stressed, overwhelmed or anxious, we are actually wired to crave sugar! The stress hormone cortisol triggers sugary food cravings which give you an instant burst of pleasure and energy. So out come the 'stress biscuits', the 'overwhelm chocolate' and the 'anxiety cake', perhaps even feeling out of control whilst eating them. You haven't lost your mind though as no matter how hard you try to override the chemicals and physiological changes in your body, you'll never win, the sugary foods will. This is why we need to address the underlying emotions much more than banning the foods.

2. Food Calms Us

Following on from the previous point, carbohydrate-rich foods (such as sugary biscuits and sugary snacks) increase the brain concentration of the amino acid called Tryptophan, which is a building block to serotonin. Serotonin is the transmitter which when released, gives us that happy feeling. It's a happy hormone. The same way we get a release of serotonin when we move our body through exercise or activity, the same is true when we overeat. So in effect whenever we reach for food as we are feeling stressed or anxious, our brain is looking for pleasure, to feel happier in that moment and to help relax our nervous system.

3. Stress affects brain function

Finally when we are stressed we often feel like we can't think straight which actually is completely true, we can't. Stress hormones of adrenaline and cortisol affect our thought process so much, especially if it is prolonged stress, that often our actions and behaviours seem 'out of control.' That would explain why on the one hand you know eating that huge cream cake might not be what your body wants, but you eat it anyway as the stress response takes over and you become mindless with your actions.

Stress is not always about jobs, money, partners, families and other external things.

Stress is often significantly self created. Obsessing about food and our bodies creates the same stress response in our body as worrying about a family member, money or an on going problem at work. That's why incorporating relaxation time into your life is so important so whether it be time outside walking, reading, meditation or something else, the more you can maintain a base line of calmness, the less likely food becomes a coping mechanism. Something for you to think about.

IN THOSE MOMENTS WE ARE TURNING TO FOOD FOR REASONS OTHER THAN PHYSICAL HUNGER. IT'S EMOTIONAL HUNGER.

To keep this really simple, there are two main reasons why we emotionally eat or binge eat

1 - It's a natural response to physical or emotional deprivation and restriction i.e. diets!

2 - We are wanting to change our emotional state; moving from feeling uncomfortable to feeling more comfortable in

that moment.

(Note: There can be a 3rd reason why a woman may binge eat and that is because she is under feeding herself. If you are a restrictor and find yourself binge eating, I urge you to be honest as to whether your body is starving for food. You cannot stop binge eating if it is happening due to your body needing food for survival and energy. If this is the case then seeking professional help is highly recommended. You'll find resources in the back of the book to help with this.)

Many women who are emotional eaters and binge eaters simply turn to food as a coping strategy to deal with life. It's undeniable that life will have ups and downs, yet it's the way we respond to these ups and downs is when food can become our best friend. Just like some people turn to drugs, alcohol, gambling, cigarettes or toxic relationships, emotional eaters turn to food when life becomes challenging or they feel uncomfortable. Arguably it's not the best long-term solution as it brings with it guilt, shame and stress but we cannot deny that food is easily accessible, socially acceptable, readily available and can work temporarily by distracting or numbing us out.

In the midst of my disordered eating, I didn't know how to deal with worry. I had no idea what to do with anxiety and no way of allowing my fears to be processed so I started to turn to food as a way of distracting myself, metaphorically and emotionally pushing those emotions down whilst also numbing out of life. It was easier for me to deal with the guilt and shame of eating an entire cake than it was to deal with the underlying fear and anxiety which I had been stuffing down and ignoring for years. Perhaps this is something which you can relate to as well?

Now in terms of binge eating, I've heard people talk about

the urge to binge as being the issue so if we simply learn to ignore the urge by no longer acting on it then binge eating will stop. Although I kind of appreciate the notion I disagree with it as not everyone has urges to binge eat, so where does the urge come from in the first place and why do we then act on it? It's exploring the reasons why and the roots of the problem where you'll find a permanent answer and solution to overcoming binge eating, rather than no longer acting on the urge to binge. Stop the urge in the first place and the whole thing collapses.

You Can't Fight Physiology

Throughout my journey of fighting food which was fuelled by the desire to lose weight, I stuck to a diet for a little while with some degree of 'success' but after falling off each diet wagon and restarting a new one, it became increasingly more difficult to prevent myself from binging. It was almost as if I had no control in the matter, regardless of how much I tried. The diet - binge - guilt - cycle became part of my normal behaviour around food which worsened over time, something my client Helen could relate to also.

HELEN: MY BINGE EATING WAS OUT OF CONTROL

....

I was very controlling with food. I would restrict my calorie intake quite extremely some days where other days I allowed myself to eat more. I had many moments of thinking there was something wrong with me as no matter how hard I tried I couldn't physically resist eating when I had the urge to do so and it was any food which I could get my hands on! It's like the more I tried to resist, the bigger the desire to binge and I wasn't even in control of my own body. I felt so powerless and it was scary at times as it truly felt completely beyond my control, it felt like I wasn't even in the driver's seat and I was being taken over by something.

Like Helen, I also didn't know back in the day that our primary reason for binging is actually rooted in the physiology of how our body works. It is something which we have little control over, despite what we think and despite what we try because willpower has nothing to do with it; binging is a physiological and normal response to any kind of physical or emotional food restriction such as dieting or calorie counting.

When your body believes there is an imminent threat of starvation or starvation is actually occurring, she does everything she can to store energy in the form of consuming more food wherever possible. You have as much conscious control of that as you do controlling your breath or stopping your heart beat. Statistically speaking, the chances of over-riding this instinctive, primitive, physiological and natural response are so small, they are practically non-existent. In fact the more we try and control our restrictions, the more powerful this physiological response becomes that before long you find yourself stood in the kitchen eating an entire packet of chocolate biscuits. I'm sure I'm not the only one that has done that and not just once.

So if you have tried to stop your binging by using willpower, by enforcing control around that behaviour in a 'I-Will-Not-Binge-Today' kind of way, I just want you to know that is never going to work. Not because there is something wrong with you but the exact opposite, because your body is so amazing at bringing herself into balance all the time.

Remember that restriction isn't only physical restriction, it can also be emotional restriction. The ways in which we view food and the stories we keep telling ourselves about food, means that over time we can become emotionally restricted such as 'I shouldn't have cake as it's not good for me' or 'I'm going to have salad instead of chips with my sandwich as I'm trying to be good.'

THE MORE YOU RESTRICT, THE MORE YOUR BODY WILL PHYSIOLOGICALLY CAUSE YOU TO BINGE.

Each of us has a shy inner rebel who makes herself known

from time to time, this is often one of those times. In the same way that if you tell a little child it can't have something or do something, they often want it or do it regardless and you do the same whenever there is emotional restriction around food choice as our natural state of being is to experience freedom in all areas of our lives. You will automatically want that food as you are rebelling against being told that you can't as your freedom of choice has been removed. Trying to be the good girl around food choice will backfire eventually as, at some point, you'll experience your inner rebel sticking her middle finger up and saying, 'sod this, I'm eating that {insert 'bad' food} and there's nothing you can do about it. You're not telling me what to do!'

THE MORE YOU TRY AND BE GOOD WITH FOOD THE MORE YOUR BODY WILL BINGE. THE MORE YOU IMPOSE ANY KIND OF EMOTIONAL RESTRICTION AROUND FOOD, THE MORE YOUR BODY WILL BINGE.

So what can you do about it? Well removing those threats of starvation and scarcity from your life is a great place to start. Stop dieting, stop food restriction and start giving yourself permission to eat whatever your body desires whilst working to improve your self trust along with strengthening your body image. There are more steps further in the book.

You are never going to win over nature and no matter how much willpower you have, it will simply never compete with the physiology of your amazing body. She's smarter than you are allowing her to be.

FEEL THE FEELS

When we numb the darkness, we also numb the light

As human beings we are constantly connected to our feelings and emotions and that is a great thing when we know how to embrace them and feel them, yet for many of us we don't.

In the quick and fast paced life in which we live, we are so used to wanting and requiring speed with everything. We want doctors to give us pills to make us better faster. We want to get our food fast. We want to surf the internet with the fastest broadband speeds possible and we also want to get over feeling the feels fast too. Moreover, we don't actually even allow ourselves to feel in the first place. Instead we have learnt to ignore, push down, disconnect and 'not go there' for fear of what we might find.

I ran away from the all too familiar unsettled and anxious feeling I had about my job, career, future and partner for years, partly because I didn't fully understand how significant they were to driving my constant struggles with food but also, there was a part of me that didn't want to go into those feelings for fear of what I'd uncover and what might happen. I was scared of the truth. I was scared of my truth. I was scared to trust myself.

It's true that the Western world doesn't equip us with the tools to truly feel how we feel, not like other parts of the globe. We have become so used to being disconnected to our bodies and our feelings that it can seem a little weird to start tuning in again.

We hate to feel anxious so we numb out of that feeling so as to avoid it. We don't like the discomfort of worry so we numb out and ignore it. We don't like the way that anger makes us feel so once again, you've guessed it, we numb out so we don't need to go there. And there are many ways of numbing out, food is just one of them. Some of us numb out with alcohol, smoking, shopping, social media, trashy tv shows, drugs, sex or any combination of these.

I've seen in my practice that women have often been shown or taught to run away from pain, to do whatever they can to avoid the hurt. We try and keep our children protected from anything which might make them feel uncomfortable and with my own children, I question whether we, as a society, are doing them a disservice as feeling that stuff is arguably inescapable. So when those little children grow up and find themselves with that pain and discomfort, it is often much easier to just flee by hitting the escape button of numbing out.

During the time when I used to fight food, I was at war with my inner world on a daily basis. Feeling anxious, worried, scared, lonely, lost and angry were the things I couldn't deal with. I didn't know how. I've come to realise over the years in which I recovered how many of us have been taught to be afraid, ashamed, embarrassed and even guilty by how we feel, often needing to play it down or justify it to others. The old fashioned stiff upper lip of being British is something which I always think of when I'm talking about this with phrases like 'just get on with it,' 'pull yourself together,' 'don't be soft,' 'stop crying' and 'be brave' so engrained into our culture.

This isn't about judging your up bringing or the people involved with that, it's simply about shining a light onto this subject to help you fully appreciate what's going on within your own story and why running away from feelings is your default response. Until now that is.

I know that feeling our feelings can be inconvenient, they can be overwhelming and they can be scary. None of us ever want to feel uncomfortable. None of us ever want to feel discomfort. None of us certainly don't ever want to feel pain but our feelings and emotions are, believe it or not, one of the most powerful aspects of ourselves which, when we learn to embrace them, allows us to truly understand, witness and explore ourselves in a way which many of us have never been shown and here is where the magic lies. Soon we'll be discussing how body wisdom is the art and skill of allowing your body to guide you when it comes to eating and physical hunger and your emotions are exactly the same. When we give ourselves permission and space to feel how we feel with no judgement or criticism, purely through the lens of curiosity, it's incredible what we start to notice.

WE CAN ALL FIND AN OPPORTUNITY FOR GROWTH WITHIN OUR OWN DISCOMFORT

Being a mum has made me appreciate how little children are so in touch with their feelings! When they are happy they show it. When they are cross, they show it. When they are sad and feeling like the world is about to end as they didn't get the right coloured spoon, they show it and I'm sure you've seen a child switch from one feeling to another instantly. Sadly we lose our ability to do this as adults, or more accurately we are taught not to do that as it's simply not what grown ups do, so instead of showing and processing how we feel (like my daughter having a tantrum when I gave her the orange spoon and not the purple one and she was so angry about it), we feed our feelings instead. We swallow them down and we stuff them back in by turning the volume down, numbing out and running away from them with a family sized bag of crisps in one hand and a bottle of wine in the other. I've spoken to many women who have told me how they would run to the fridge whenever they felt a sense of overwhelm or fear, knowing full well they were beginning to feel uncomfortable but distracting themselves with whatever they could eat.

Emotions are something which are just part of being human and the more we are either taught or believe it's not ok to have these feelings, the more distant we become from our truth of how we honestly feel for it's our inner wisdom trying to guide us towards our next steps. I now see feelings and emotions as being our own internal guidance system which is showing us what is needing and requiring our attention at any given moment. Use your emotions like incredibly intricate internal compasses because when you feel overwhelmed there is a reason for it, when you feel scared there is a reason for it and the same for anger and any other emotion. So rather than saying to yourself, 'I don't want to feel that so I'm going to ignore it, pretend it doesn't exist or stuff it down with a piece of cake,' what if you could sit with that emotion and follow it on it's journey and see where it takes you?

WHEN YOU MOVE THROUGH THE FEELING YOU WILL GAIN CLARITY ON SOMETHING.

If you feel anxious in your job, could it be because that's not the right job for you?
If you feel unsettled with your partner, could it be that something needs to change?
If you feel angry towards someone, could it be that you need to redefine your boundaries? Sadly most of us don't ever explore the reason for how we feel because we are too busy stuffing our faces with biscuits, crisps and cake whilst beating ourselves up in the process for eating 'bad' food.

When we become more self aware and can appreciate that food, up until now, has been this symbolic coping strategy allowing us to numb out of our own reality, we can start to take our power back and create a life which empowers us, lights us up and makes us feel good. There is also nothing fundamentally wrong with you feeding your feelings at the moment. I did this for 14 years. However, what I have learnt is that in order to move through life feeling balanced, in control and actually happier, we have to get to a place where we can put on our big girl pants and start being honest with why we are feeling like we are and then taking responsibility and aligned action in whatever form we can.

I know that at the end of the day we are trying to protect ourselves by becoming selective at what we choose to feel and what we choose to ignore but the truth is that we cannot be selective when it comes to our feelings.

If you are avoiding feeling anxious, you'll also be unable to feel true happiness.
If you are avoiding feeling lonely, you'll also be unable to feel true joy.
If you are avoiding feeling angry, you'll also be unable to feel true contentment.

AS SOON AS WE TURN DOWN THE FEELS, WE TURN THEM ALL DOWN

When you start your own journey of finding food freedom, ditching the diet rules and learning to listen to yourself again, those feelings you have habitually turned down and ignored through food, will still be there, so what happens?

You learn, one step at a time, to start feeling them and no longer run away and feed them. There is nothing wrong with you if you feel angry. There is nothing wrong with you if you feel upset. There is nothing wrong with you if you feel scared, anxious or afraid. You are normal, completely normal and the faster you can appreciate that, the better.

JO: MY BINGE EATING WAS OUT OF CONTROL

....

Growing up I witnessed my parents arguing all the time. My dad was a very loud man and often raised his voice when he got cross, to the point of it terrifying me. I remember feeling so scared when he was in one of those moods which didn't happen that often, but when it did it was horrible. I never fully appreciated how I saw anger as being something bad and scary and I did whatever I could to never get angry when I grew up. I know now that anger can be a healthy emotion when expressed in a healthy way and I'm finding ways of doing that for myself now.

How do you handle your feelings and emotions? What do you do with them? What have you been shown growing up on addressing how you feel? We often learn how to process and handle our feelings based on watching others such as our family in particular and like Jo, we can create association to some emotions which we can carry with us into adulthood.

Perhaps you were never shown how to express your emotions growing up or you were exposed to emotions which were overwhelming and scary so you avoid them as an adult through fear of feeling them again. Maybe emotions like anger, guilt or shame were never mentioned or discussed within your family which is common for so many and here is where the problem lies. When we assume that how we feel is wrong or 'not good', it's easy to see why we can become very closed off to what's going on from our neck down. Ironically, isn't it interesting how our emotions are felt in our bodies, yet most women who struggle with body insecurities and who fight food, ignore what's going on from their neck down? That's not a coincidence. If you cut yourself off from your body, you cut off from your emotions or is it the other way around? Dropping down into our bodies can feel really uncomfortable and for some women really unsafe especially if you have spent a long time believing that your body is broken, is not good enough or has somehow let you down, you might initially struggle to trust what she's showing you and what feelings she's giving off but stay with it. Use the resources in this book to help you.

I compare emotions to being like coloured smoke inside a glass bottle. Ideally we need to loosen the cork and let that smoke out otherwise it becomes too smoky in there, we can't see clearly anymore and the pressure begins to build. Yet many of us don't do that. We notice the smoke or feel the emotion and then tighten the cork in fear of any of it escaping or coming out and during the whole time we are doing that, it's getting smokier inside that glass bottle until eventually it's too much, the pressure builds and blows the cork out all by itself.

When we don't express our emotions by loosening that metaphorical cork, they stay trapped inside, changing and manifesting over time. Emotions such as guilt and shame will begin to eat you from the inside if you do not express or process them, so stuffing them down with food is never going to make them go away, it will just prolong your suffering. I became an expert at ignoring my feelings. An expert at stuffing them down with handfuls of food and pretending I was ok, holding that facade of everything was fine on the outside, yet inside was a different story. Anxiety, overwhelm and later panic attacks started to become normal day occurrences and the bigger they got, the more I ate. Having to face up to the truth and feel those feelings within myself was so uncomfortable that I checked out and changed the channel so as not to acknowledge what was brewing inside.

There's also something else which I want to mention which is we often deflect the original emotion back onto blaming our bodies. Here's what I mean. You notice you feel anxious and that is something which you don't want to feel, so you go into the kitchen and eat whatever you can as your coping strategy has once again been reactivated as you find yourself in a whirlwind of food, eating and feeling as if you have lost control. Then what happens? Eventually you stop and notice that you feel so bad and guilty about what you just did as you promised yourself you wouldn't do that again. So there you are, feeling ashamed, disgusted and annoyed with yourself and your focus comes back to your body and your weight, not the original emotion which triggered the whole thing.

As crazy as it sounds, it's often easier to feel the guilt of overeating than it is to feel the anxiety in the first place. Or the loneliness. Or the panic. Those initial emotions sometimes seem so big and so overwhelming that we don't know what to do with them, so it's easier to push them down with a giant bar of chocolate and then deal with the subsequent guilt and shame which ensue.

Allowing yourself to feel anxious and explore the reasons why is not comfortable, of course it isn't, yet stuffing that feeling of anxiety down with food is also not comfortable and it's also never going to help you in the long run. Only by stepping into your truth and acknowledging how you feel can any of us become truly free from food obsession and ultimately become reconnected back to who we are.

EXERCISE #1: FEELING YOUR FEELINGS

....

I invite you to become curious around the emotions and feelings which you have, even though I know that these feelings can make you feel uncomfortable. No-one wants to sit in the emotions of anxiety, overwhelm, fear or panic but what most of us do is not even sit in it for a millisecond, we shove it down with food, we switch it off, we detach ourselves and get even more busy so we don't have to acknowledge what's there. Yet by doing that over and over again, we separate ourselves from our soul hunger, we don't listen and we become disembodied women who are certainly not soul fed.

I invite you to start being honest with yourself from now. Next time you turn to food in a way you know or suspect is for stuffing something down or distraction, take a few deep breaths and ask yourself out of curiosity.....

How do I feel? If you can't label what you are aware of, that's fine. Just bring your attention to what you notice.
What am I aware of?
Can I sit with this for a minute or so? If not, why?
What am I making this feeling mean?
Where in my body can I feel it?
What does it remind me of?
What am I really swallowing down?
If I wasn't eating this, what would I need to acknowledge?
What might I be running away from?

Use some tapping to help with whatever comes up for you. You don't have to share any of this with anyone but you need to be honest with yourself.

EXERCISE #2: YOU ARE NOT THE EMOTION

Language is powerful. Become aware of how you talk about your feelings.

For example, saying 'I am so anxious right now' has much more power over you than saying 'I am feeling this emotion of anxiety, I wonder why?'

Can you feel the difference? One is attached to you and you are making it yours whilst the other is from a place of observation, curiosity and taking your power back.

EMOTIONS ARE STUCK IN FOOD

So we've established that turning to food for reasons other than physical hunger is, more often than not, about wanting to change your emotional state. However, there is also a little bit more to this and it's about the types of food which you turn to in those situations. I very rarely come across someone who tells me she binges on mangos or that apples are her food of choice when she is emotionally eating! Instead it's more likely to be ice cream, bread, pasta, cakes, chocolate, cheese and any other kind of comfort food. I bet you've never realised but emotions can actually become stuck in foods. I want to share with you something which, even after years of working with the mind, it blows me away how clever it can be.

We have a fascinatingly intricate wiring in our minds, literally absorbing every bit of information around us every second of the day which often becomes hard wired as neurological pathways in our minds, forming our beliefs, behaviours and habits. We do the same with food. We record emotions and memories associated with food which become hard wired on a subconscious level, meaning we aren't even aware of these programs running.

I want to ask you to think of a food which you often find difficult to resist. What food do you turn to when you've had a bad day or feel anxious? What are the foods which you overeat on? What about the foods which you can quite easily binge on whenever you are needing that 'fix'. What are your trigger foods or 'go-to' foods?

For me it was always cake. Any kind. Any flavour. It didn't matter. There was something about the texture, taste and the way I felt whilst eating it that made cake my nemesis for years. Think about one of your go-to foods. Have you got any positive and lovely memories associated with eating that food in the past? Are there any particular people associated with that food when you think about it? I'm going to take a wild guess that most of those memories involve people who you care about, who made you feel loved, safe and appreciated and they were happy times. Am I right? This is where emotions become trapped in the food and no matter how much we try and resist eating that food, we can't as we are literally being controlled by subconscious programming which consciously is very difficult to override.

A former client of mine, Pamela, has this story to share:

PAMELA: MY LOVE FOR ICE CREAM

....

My parents divorced when I was 6 and my brother and I used to visit our dad every other weekend. He was and still is a great dad and despite my parents divorcing, our relationship was thankfully never affected. He always used to take us to this old fashioned ice cream parlour when we visited and he let us have whatever we liked. It was our treat which we looked forward to all week! I have very fond memories of myself and my brother giggling being surrounded with these gigantic ice cream sundaes which felt bigger than our heads at the time whilst dad was being silly and laughing with us.

Guess what Pamela's go to food was when she was emotionally eating and which she could quite easily binge on?

Ice cream. Always ice cream.

Why?

Well her mind had hard wired ice cream with the association of her dad's love, safety, happiness and fun. So is it any wonder whenever she felt lonely, fed up or down she was on auto pilot wanting ice cream?

The truth is though, she didn't actually want the ice cream. In that moment her mind was scanning all ways of accessing those feelings of happiness, fun and feeling loved, literally changing her emotional state and ice cream was the thing it found. The same way that my thing was cake. My mum was always baking (she still does) and the emotions in that cake of love, comfort and safety was what my mind was seeking whenever I felt anything but safe or happy. I've heard so many different stories around food types over the years from diet drinks to chocolate bars along with traditional family favourites.

GISELLE: MY ITALIAN FAMILY

....

I'm Italian and I grew up in a traditional and typical Italian family. I remember how mum was always in the kitchen preparing food, making pasta and cooking for us, food was very much at the centre of the home. Several times throughout the week we'd have a huge Italian style meal with my aunties, uncles and cousins too and I remember the house smelling amazing of fresh pasta, basil and tomatoes. It was really typically Italian with plates of food coming out of the kitchen. My mum's pasta making was well known and she's still a fabulous cook, far better than I've ever become!

So what was Giselle's binge food?

Pasta and bowls of the stuff!

Funnily enough Giselle had tried to eat carb free many times and never succeeded. She was literally taking out the food (pasta) which was associated with feeling good, happy, loved, safe and cared for, no wonder she became more than irritated and angry when she was no longer allowed to eat it.

I've helped so many women take the emotion out of food by sending it back where it came from through reprogramming their emotional association to the food. By doing that ice cream becomes ice cream, cake becomes cake and pasta becomes pasta.

Ok so let's move on. It's time to take your power back gorgeous lady!

STEP FOUR:
DITCH THE DIETS

TAKE YOUR POWER BACK

Whenever we stay attached to diet culture through our behaviours it makes finding our freedom more difficult than it needs to be.

Hopefully, having read this far, you can appreciate how dieting and diet culture has been adding fuel to this fire and finding your food freedom and ending this battle begins when you deliberately take steps towards ditching those diets once and for all.

How do you feel about that? Do you feel excited, lighter, curious or perhaps intrigued? Or do you feel slightly anxious, worried or maybe even petrified at the thought of no longer relying on your diets in the way that you have done previously?

Most women experience a complete mix of emotions when they have that realisation that in order to find their freedom they need to say goodbye to the diet rules which they have leant on for so long. Whether you feel happy at leaving your diet club, shocked at how on earth that's going to work or hysterical with fear that there will be no more rules or guidelines, it's going to be ok.

I frequently get asked 'how on earth do I ditch the diets when I don't trust myself with food?!?!' The idea for many of us is terrifying and can fill us with fear yet at the same time, the idea of no longer being a dieter also excites us and gives us a small glimmer of liberation and freedom! The truth is that often the fear we have at the thought of ditching the diets is not only a completely normal reaction but it's actually not a bad thing for it's keeping us safe or at least trying to.

Having fought food for years, it would be understandable to find it challenging to imagine a life where food doesn't control you and so you stick with what you know, believing that diets keep you safe as if they are some kind of security blanket protecting you from the biscuit tin and other non-diet friendly foods. You start to believe that without diets you will completely lose your control when it comes to eating. You start to believe that without the plans and programs and other eating guidelines, you would end up eating yourself into oblivion and overnight become the size of the house! You start to think that you cannot trust yourself around certain foods so by putting yourself on a diet you'll have more self control because you are being told what to eat, when to eat and how much to eat.

THE IRONY IS THAT DIETING DOESN'T HELP YOU HAVE MORE CONTROL AROUND FOOD.

DIETS TAKE YOUR CONTROL AWAY.

I'll be completely honest with you that initially when you step away from the diet plans you might think you're free falling with no safety net, except that isn't true. Diets are not your safety net and never have been for they do not give you more control around food. They do not keep you safe and they do not protect you from your lack of willpower. What diets are incredibly good at doing is fuelling the bingeing, feeding emotional eating and encouraging the food and weight obsession. Diets have very little impact on improving your self control around food and actually they're causing you to lose control around food far more than if you didn't diet in the first place!

In the times you have fallen off the diet wagon, I am guessing that you've overeaten, binged and lost control around the non-diet foods, haven't you? And you do that because you know at some point in the near future, possibly at the beginning of next week, you will restart the diet again in order to try and bring more control to your eating behaviours. Yet whilst you were waiting for that diet to re-start once more you find yourself losing control with food.

I'm going to ask you again, do you honestly think that diets are keeping you safe from losing control with food or are they causing the issue?

THE MORE WE TRY AND CONTROL FOOD, THE MORE IT CONTROLS US.

THE PERFECT WAY TO EAT

I used to like the thrill of seeing the numbers come down when I was eating 'perfectly' and sticking to the plans. I felt successful at weight loss initially because my perfectionism and low self esteem made me feel inadequate and not enough in so many other areas of my life and therein lay a huge problem. I didn't appreciate how perfection is the disguise of insecurity and it's one I see all the time in dysfunctional eaters.

A desire to find the perfect way to eat.

I used to think I'd ruined my entire day if I ate something which I wasn't supposed to. It would be enough for me to just carry on eating and eating and eating. Sometimes for hours. Sometimes for days. Sometimes for even longer.

Saying we've ruined it all and then binging for the rest of the day happens frequently to most dieters and it's a bizarre behaviour which I think all of us can identify with, but if you dropped your phone on the floor, you wouldn't think 'oh I might as well stamp on it now and smash the screen until it's broken and then get it repaired tomorrow' would you? Yet we do it every time we aren't eating perfectly by beating ourselves up and then turning to food to comfort ourselves for feeling like we've messed it all up. It's crazy! I'm a recovering perfectionist as occasionally I have to catch myself trying to be 'perfect' in some area of my life and I thankfully very rarely slip into that place anymore, certainly no where near as frequently as I used to as I recognised that if I truly wanted to end the 14 year self destructive cycle I had been in, I had to be willing to let go of trying to be perfect.

Are you willing to admit that your search for perfectionism often leads to self-abuse, stress and overwhelm?

Perfectionists have such high expectations of themselves and those standards are often unrealistic that they can spend their lives living by 'I should"....

- I should go to the gym today

- I should be eating according to this diet/eating plan

- I should lose 10lbs then I'd feel better

- I really should try harder

I want to invite you to explore your own need for perfectionism. Something I'd like to highlight is every single one of us is perfectly imperfect and always will be and that's what makes us who we are. Being a perfectionist with all these standards and expectations is not only exhausting but when you believe your body should be a certain size or shape and you should be eating perfectly all the time then you set yourself up on this hamster wheel of never feeling good enough.

IF YOU SEEK PERFECTIONISM IN ANY AREA OF YOUR LIFE, YOU WILL CONTINUOUSLY FEEL LIKE YOU'VE FAILED.

Interestingly women who are self-proclaimed perfectionists are more likely to develop disordered eating behaviours due to the nature of their own imposed high expectations and their right versus wrong attitude to life. My professional experience can confirm that to be true, pretty much 100% of all the women I have ever worked with have been perfectionists with an 'all or nothing' approach to food like Hannah.

HANNAH: STRAIGHT 'A' STUDENT

....

I was a perfectionist most of my life. I managed to get straight A's throughout my entire education as I refused to settle for anything less. Yet as I got older and felt like I was in competition with the other people in the company I worked for, the high achieving perfectionist within me applied this same attitude towards my work which created lots of stress and overwhelm but also to my nutrition, which I believe led me to develop the disordered eating habits I had for years. I was either eating good or eating bad, there was no happy medium. It really was an all or nothing approach to how I was doing food.

If you carry around the feelings of failure as you ate some cake and your Paleo diet says you can't have it or feeling that you are a failure as you said you'd go to the gym 5 times this week but only managed 3, life is going to be pretty crap, not to mention your self esteem will take a beating and how you feel about yourself will certainly not improve. You may even find yourself reaching for the 'comfort' biscuits or the 'feeling sorry for myself' ice-cream....then the whole cycle starts again.

PERFECTIONISTS IRONICALLY DON'T SEE HOW IMPERFECT THE PRACTICE OF PERFECTIONISM ACTUALLY IS

So many women are on the quest to find the perfect diet and the perfect way to eat, believing it will lead to their perfect weight, perfect skin and perfect life, often searching for years trying to find it and every once in a while jumping into something believing that will be it. The excitement is always short lived though when their cravings and binging gets the better of them. Whether it be Paleo, Atkins, sugar free, wheat free, diary free, vegetarianism, vegan or Keto, they are never 'perfect' for anyone.

To quote Marc David, founder of the Institute for the Psychology of Eating, '*The desire for perfection in any area of life is a form of simplistic wishful thinking. It's a way of approaching the world that calls for more maturity and experience. Perfectionism is a dream that we need to wake up from. The alternative is to continue sleepwalking and not understand why we're constantly feeling off-balance, disempowered, uncertain, and always looking for answers about why our health or our eating habits aren't perfect.*'

Believing there is one size fits all when it comes to eating puts us in a position where we overlook some really important points. We can find ourselves becoming stressed, anxious and worried about what we should be eating basing all of our decisions and actions around our 'perfect' diet, turning down invitations for lunch or social events as they aren't compatible with our choice to eat the way we currently are based on the plan we have chosen at any given point in time. And if we do find a way to eat which we believe is 'perfect' it always results in us 'falling off the wagon' by craving and binging on foods which aren't allowed on that 'perfect' diet like the time I ate an entire cake 3 weeks into Atkins as I was desperate for sugar and carbs!

If we take a step away from food and eating though for a moment, I'd like to ask you if there are any other areas in life where there is a perfect way of doing them? A perfect way to bring up children? Clean a house? Be in a marriage or a relationship? A perfect way to have sex, have fun or move your body? Of course there isn't. So why should eating be any different? Finding a way which is right for your body which nourishes her physically, emotionally and spiritually is multidimensional. It's dependent on the seasons, the amount of sleep you've had, your age, your hormones, your job, your activity levels and your emotional state. One size can not ever fit all despite what you've been told.

Yet don't panic. Before you find yourself slipping into a state of overwhelm, just stop and keep breathing. The world of nutrition is conflicting, confusing, complicated and down right messy at the best of times, so here's what I did when I started walking away from the rules and, in fact, this is what I still do.

Stop. Listen. Explore. Trust.

When you let the pursuit go of searching for the perfect way to eat, an amazing thing happens. You relax. Mind, body & soul. I believe that our bodies really do know exactly what they need and when. Sometimes you may need more carbs to keep your body nourished. Sometimes you might need more vegetables or fruit. Sometimes it could be more meat or fish. Sometimes she may ask for sweetness. I completely trust my body and allow her to have a piece of cake for breakfast if that's what she desires as I know she'll tell me when she needs something more nutritious and she often does (not that cake is wrong, no food choice is ever wrong, we're coming to that bit soon.) I suggest you try and buy the best of everything by the way. If your body wants chocolate make sure it's Belgian and rich. If your body wants steak, get the best cut you can. It makes all the difference when we nourish ourselves with quality as it's connected to feeling satisfied whilst eating.

EXERCISE: DROP THE PERFECTION

....

How much of a perfectionist are you?

How often do you try and do everything as perfectly as possible?

How much pressure do you put on yourself to get everything right or have/do anything in a certain way?

In what areas of your life could you drop the need for perfection?

Reconnect To Body Wisdom

There is a voice which doesn't use words. Listen. - Rumi

However you feel about the thought of ditching the diet is completely normal. You are normal. Your emotions and feelings to this topic are all completely normal and you have every reason to feel how you do, likely a combination of everything. So the next logical question you probably have is...... *how on earth do I do this?*

Well it's not difficult to cancel diet memberships. To throw away diet books. To get rid of diet plans. To let go of all diet paraphernalia from in and around your home but then what? How do you eat? What do you eat? Where do you even begin?

Let's start with a really important place. Body wisdom.

What does body wisdom mean to you? What do you understand by that term?

The easiest way of explaining body wisdom is to imagine reconnecting your head back to your body! Emotionally, energetically and spiritually opening up that connection and communication with everything from your neck down as you've possibly spent a lifetime being disconnected from her (your body) by fighting food, ignoring your hungers, not trusting her and eating based on plans, programs and the clock. Anyone who struggles with any of these topics we have discussed so far must be, by definition, disconnected from their body, disconnected from themselves and disconnected from their truth.

LOUISA: COMPLETELY DETACHED

....

From the moment I woke up in the morning and before I'd even got out of bed, I was already thinking about breakfast and what I should have. Quite often that would be based on the previous day's eating behaviour and whether or not I had been good or bad with my food. The rest of my day was pretty much no different. Thoughts around lunch, thoughts around afternoon snacks, thoughts around my dinner in the evening and also spending some of that time and energy working out calories, fat or protein, depending on what diet or eating program I was on. I hadn't realised how disconnected I had become to myself and my body. I had turned eating into an intellectual challenge and never once listened to what my body was telling me.

Turning eating into a 'head thing' is what dysfunctional eaters do. They 'think' about what to eat and when to eat by planning, plotting and overanalysing food constantly. The more we move our focus into our head, we detach from ourselves and start relying more and more on external guides and programs which tell us how and what to eat. This moves us further and further away from our natural and innate ability to know, to listen and tune in and allow our incredible body to guide us.

If you truly want to find your food freedom and heal your relationship with food and yourself, then connecting back to your body through body wisdom is arguably one of the most important and pivotal steps on this journey. When we reconnect to our body wisdom, we are tuning back into the fundamental and natural way that we, as human beings, have been programmed to eat. Tuning back into our instinct. Our inner knowing. Our self trust. Our intuition. The way we were born into this world as small babies before society taught us that our hungers and bodies couldn't be trusted.

Small children are a prime example of being aware of body wisdom. When my children were toddlers, it was fascinating to watch them interact with food. They instinctively knew what to do. They knew when they were hungry, they would only eat what they enjoyed and they would always leave food when they had eaten enough or asked for more if there wasn't enough to satisfy them. So isn't it interesting how despite the fact that each and everyone of us was born with body wisdom and this natural and instinctive knowledge of how to eat, that the majority of us end up losing it as we grow older? Dieting is significantly responsible for this without question.

Think about how amazing our bodies are at letting us know things. We know when we are thirsty, when we are tired or when we need the toilet, non of which we question, and it's exactly the same for when we need food for energy and to nourish ourselves, that is until we get on the diet wagon. Diets train us to override hunger and wait until the next allowed meal based on the clock. Diets teach us to ignore our body signals in order to fit with the plan. Diets encourage us to tune out of our body wisdom on so many levels and by doing so we stop trusting ourselves.

Although I believe that dieting is arguably the biggest reason why we disconnect from ourselves, stress and general life do also play a role too. When we are too busy rushing from one thing to the next, it's easy to ignore hunger in the moment but then suddenly find ourselves inhaling whatever we can get our hands on due to feeling ravenous and needing to eat anything. How often has that happened to you? And the same is true on the other end of the spectrum too, eating when our bodies aren't asking for food as food is being used for emotional reasons, support, comfort and love as we've previously been discussing. Often we are quick to make food choice decisions based on habit, based on fear, based on conditioning and based on brain washing, yet the fact of the matter is, that often, those food choices are not what your body wants to eat. If you asked her she'd probably tell you something different.

'So how do I reconnect to my body wisdom?!' I hear you screaming at the page!

I want to keep this super simple, there is no need to overcomplicate this topic at all. In fact we could argue that you have been over complicating this activity for far too many years already. When we spend all of our time and energy in our head we are disconnected from ourselves. In order to reconnect to her, your amazing and wonderful self, your energy has got to be in your body. You have to be home. Don't assume you know the answers by the way. Ask her. Talk to her. Sit with her for a while. I know this sounds really out there but it isn't. It's about you starting to reconnect with yourself and learning to trust what you hear. You will find some help with this in the bonus resources which come with the book, head over to www.soulfedwoman.com/bookbonuses

EXERCISE: CONNECTING TO BODY WISDOM

....

I recommend you practise this exercise multiple times a day. You can do it anywhere, nobody will know that you are doing it and the more that you make this a new habit, the art of body wisdom will become much easier. Whenever you find yourself in your head, thinking about something or over analysing something or milling something over, recognise that you're doing it without judgement or criticism and then simply move your attention downwards.

Imagine a ball of light just below your belly button deep within you. This is your centre. Imagine that ball of light as real as you can. Perhaps you can feel it, perhaps you have an awareness of it or perhaps you set the intention that it is simply there. And that's all you need to do. It sounds ridiculously simple doesn't it? And indeed it is in many ways. Start directing your thoughts and therefore your energy down into your centre, down into your body and away from your head.

Reconnecting to your body and to body wisdom is practically impossible if you are never in your body in the first place. So I highly recommend that you get into the habit of practising this ball of light exercise multiple times a day. And on a side note this doesn't just help with improving your relationship to food, it's impact is far greater than that. The more present within our bodies we become, the more in tune with our instinct we are, the more we build our self trust muscle, the more confident we become, the less anxiety and worry we have and the more we begin to have a positive outlook on life in general. Now who wouldn't want that?

Finally for those of you saying or thinking that your body wisdom might be broken or on stand by mode, think about it this way; you've been ignoring your body for years. Not listening to her. Telling her to be quiet. Being unkind to her. Saying nasty things to her. She may be slightly hesitant to start talking to you after all of that so be patient with her and keep talking to her anyway.

I promise she'll start talking back.

Removing All The Labels

Categorising food is detrimental to feeling and being free.

Do you think about certain foods as being good or bad? Maybe healthy or not healthy? What about clean or not clean? Invisible labels are present on everything and unknowingly you have been adding labels to food for years.

Let's get one thing clear here. Food choice is not a moral issue but the diet industry has added morality to food choice for most of us. Regardless of what you order in a restaurant or what you choose to eat at lunchtime does not make you a good person or a bad person. If the friend that you are with orders something different to you, it does not mean that she is somehow better based on her food choice and you are somehow a failure based on yours. This obsessive ritual of shame and self loathing whilst eating is something which has become far too normal within our body obsessed society. Food doesn't have morality and regardless of what you choose to eat and the amount which you choose to eat, this means nothing about who you are as a person and never at any point do you need to give an excuse or apologise for what you are eating. As a grown woman who is intelligent and knows her own mind, you get to eat what ever the hell you like, so next time you are in the coffee shop don't tell the barista you shouldn't have a muffin as you order one, just order one! Stop providing justification or a reason for doing so.

Now where does labelling come in to this? Well when we deny ourselves certain foods based on their label as they are perceived as being bad, unhealthy or not clean, there is a rebellious part of us which wants those foods. This behaviour can be seen on diets. As soon as you know you aren't allowed to eat bread as you're carb-free, you either desperately crave bread the entire time you are trying to be 'good' or you binge on bread the night before your diet starts as you know you aren't allowed it from tomorrow! And as the weeks go by, you eat the foods allowed on the diet but then you start craving food you aren't allowed. You catch yourself thinking about warm buttered toast, dreaming about hot chocolate fudge cake with ice-cream and obsessing about extra mature cheddar cheese with crackers! Being in that state of mind will inevitably lead you to inhaling the 'bad food' in excessive quantities leaving you feeling guilty although perhaps not enough to stop. You've fallen off the diet at this point, so you might as well carry on eating all the 'bad' food whilst you psyche yourself up to go back on the diet again. This is usually either when you've built up enough willpower or when all the bad food has been eaten out of the kitchen cupboards. Which ever comes first. Sound familiar? This cycle can be broken by removing the labels and stopping the categorisation of food in the first place!

CRAVINGS, BINGING AND 'FALLING OFF DIETS' ARE ALL DUE TO THIS GOOD VERSUS BAD FOOD THINKING.
STOP THE THINKING AND YOU STOP THE CRAVINGS, BINGING AND 'FALLING OFF DIETS' MENTALITY

Remember food is not right or wrong. Food is not good or bad. Food does not make you a good or a bad person. Food is just food. Food is neutral. Some food choices may be more nutritious than others but that doesn't make them any better in anyway yet when we eat anything which we perceive as being 'bad' we will naturally feel bad about ourself. Think of how you eat so called 'bad' foods at the moment. Rushed, hurried, gulping it down without even tasting it? When we eat anything whilst feeling guilty, we also eat the emotion too which affects our body's ability to digest and assimilate the food and also how we taste the food. Eating a croissant for breakfast whilst seeing it as being 'wrong' will taste very different to when you eat that croissant will full permission as you've removed the label you've given it. Eating a croissant which we no longer see as being a bad food, allows us to experience that ritual with complete pleasure and enjoyment, which leads us to having a far more positive experience of eating it in the first place. I've lost count of how many clients over the years have reported how different food tastes when they have removed the labels. Interestingly studies have also shown when we eat without labels, we naturally eat less as we know that food is available to us at anytime for it is no longer 'bad' or 'wrong' or out of bounds.

Listen gorgeous lady! You are a grown, smart and wonderful woman who is old enough and wise enough to be allowed to eat whatever you want, whenever you want it. It's all about choice so from now give yourself permission to choose everything you eat, not because you have to or because you think you should but because you choose to and you desire to.

EXERCISE: TAKE THE LABELS AWAY

....

Find a quiet spot and list all of your bad foods, the food which you have stuck an invisible label on over the years.

Don't hold yourself back with this list write them all down.

If you don't know where to start, think about the foods which you deliberately don't have at home as you think you can't trust yourself around them. The foods which practically call your name if they are in the kitchen cupboard. What are the foods which you avoid walking past in the supermarket in fear of buying them all and eating them all in the process or the foods which make you feel guilty if you eat them?

To get you started, common perceived 'bad' foods are typically things like chocolate, cake, biscuits, cheese, cream, bread, pasta, crackers, cereal etc

Now as my intention for this book is to really help you challenge your behaviours, beliefs and ultimately find your food freedom, what do you think I might ask you to do now with this list? I think you already know!

Next time you go shopping, I invite you to buy some of those things on that list. I am giving you permission to buy what ever the hell you like next time you go to the supermarket. I'm giving you permission to buy the foods which you have tried your best to avoid over the years and in doing so find you lose control whenever you are near them. I'm giving you permission to start the process of de-categorising food by removing their invisible labels.

I know you feel anxious and possibly a little bit sick at the thought of having chocolate in your kitchen but I promise you there is a very valid reason why I am asking you to do this. Those foods which you have written down on your list, even though this was never your intention, have now been put on pedestals. They're out of bounds. Not allowed. You can't have them and as soon as we put anything out of reach whilst also telling ourselves that we are not allowed them, we rebel against ourselves and those rules, leading to food cravings, food obsession, overeating and binge eating. So can you see why you have to start removing the labels in order to start taking your power back?

The only thing that I will say is please make sure that you choose food on your list which you really like. These are for you after all. So don't choose the chocolate biscuits because you think your children will like them, choose the chocolate biscuits which you know that you like. Choose the flavour of crisps which you like, not the ones which your partner does. You will see further on in the book why permission and food choice is so important when it comes to satisfaction and this begins with you buying these products for *yourself* with *full permission*.

Just incase you are panicking as you think you may eat the entire contents of your shopping trolley before you've even got to the car, I'm asking you to put your fear to one side for now and start trusting in the process. De-categorising food goes hand-in-hand with reconnecting to your body wisdom, which means that you are free to eat what ever you like whilst listening to your body. If she wants croissants for breakfast go with it. If she wants left over curry for breakfast go with it! If she doesn't want anything around 'breakfast time' go with that too. There are no rules anymore.

Before we move on I need to say one more thing though. I do not want you to approach this way of eating as a new diet. These are not rules, they are simply suggestions and things to bring into your awareness for you to explore and deepen through curiosity. Although it's very beneficial to eat based on physical hunger as much as you can, it's also completely okay to eat sometimes when you're not physically hungry. Either way giving yourself permission is key. So in the meantime pay attention to your body, open up communication with her and give yourself permission to eat what ever she tells you she desires whenever she desires it.

SWITCHING OFF DIET MENTALITY

Do you remember what we said all kinds of diets and eating regimes have in common?

They are all based around rules.

Now I don't know about you, but food rules suck. Some rules are incredibly important in life such as 'don't cross the road when a car is coming' or 'don't stick your hand in the oven when it's lit' but rules which take away joy, pleasure, fun and freedom of choice whilst pressing pause on your life, those rules I can live without. Part of finding your food freedom and really letting go of all that food noise, is very much about stepping away from diets, yet for many of us, it's not just the diet plans which are contributing to our issues, it's our diet mentality.

Diet mentality or the diet gremlin appears as soon as you have had any kind of experience with conventional dieting. It's the way that you start to create emotional attachment to the way you are eating, turning eating into a moral issue. You feel good for eating salad and bad for eating cake. I often hear women say that they don't diet yet they find themselves binging, emotional eating and stressing about what they should and shouldn't be doing with food. On closer conversation, it's the way that they are choosing to think about food needs to be addressed and ultimately changed. For example, have you ever gone to a cafe and ordered a skinny latte? Is that because it's the low fat option? Have you ever ordered a sandwich and asked for salad instead of chips? Again is that because it's the healthier option? Maybe you've omitted the salad dressing as you think that's better for you.

All of these behaviours have some kind of morality attached to them don't they?

If you order a normal full fat latte, you might feel guilty. If you ordered chips with your sandwich you might spend the entire time whilst eating wishing that you hadn't and worrying about the calories you've consumed and if you had a creamy caesar dressing on your salad, you'd think about it for a little while afterwards wishing you hadn't.

This is diet thinking or diet mentality and very clearly the work of the diet gremlin.

Now there is nothing wrong with ordering a salad instead of chips or ordering a low fat latte. The point I am making is really inviting you to be honest with yourself and find out what the motivation is behind that choice. Ordering anything based on it being better, healthier or less calorific could be connected straight back to diet mentality and what you have been conditioned to think. It implies if you don't order that way, you've made the wrong choice.

So why is this important to let go of?

Quite simply normal eaters don't think this way.

They order food based on what they want and not based on what they think they should want. Whether that's low fat, full fat, with or without chips, their desire to choose is never motivated by anything other than their desire.

If you have emotional attachment to eating in a certain way, you have diet mentality.

Ditching the diet is not difficult - you turn your back on the rules and programs - yet getting rid of diet thinking is arguably a little more challenging (not impossible though) as many women have spent years and years telling themselves that the skinny latte is the best option, that chips are not healthy and salad should be eaten only with low fat dressing or, better still, dressing free.

I want to ask you to become really aware of diet thinking from now on. In order to change anything the very first step is about recognition. Without you being aware of when your diet gremlin appears it's far more challenging to start letting this behaviour go as ditching diet thinking is about learning to change your thoughts. Now before you go into overwhelm or panic, I invite you to start having compassion around this topic. It is likely you may be shocked as to how much you think about food in a negative and judgemental way, making you feel uncomfortable, but keep observing and allowing your body wisdom to guide you.

As soon as you start judging yourself or criticising what you are noticing, you are setting yourself up to restart that all too familiar cycle of self hate. That is what you have been doing for years and it's clear to say it hasn't helped you much so it's time to change the record and start doing something different instead.

I want to encourage you to start being honest with yourself and diving a little deeper into your thoughts around food. Open up that communication with your body again. Should you recognise that you are thinking about food through the lens of diet mentality, start digging deeper. Ask yourself whether that thought is serving you. Why is it there? Where did it come from? Is it fact or assumption? Can I choose to change it? Do I have to believe it? How does it feel? Is it your diet gremlin or is it something else?

STEPHANIE: SO MANY RULES!

....

Breaking the diet rules I had unknowingly created or believed was a huge step in my recovery. I hadn't realised how many fear based rules I had been living by for years. I started breaking them one by one, not through rebellion but from the viewpoint of taking my power back. Food had controlled me for such a long time at this point and I could see why. I started eating carbs after 6pm, I would allow myself to eat cake when I fancied it and I started mixing protein and carbs together at lunch. It wasn't always easy to switch the thoughts off but it's got so much better since I started.

Hang on though, what about making food choices which are indeed better for our health?

As we've already discussed health is multidimensional, however, when we are making choices aligned with our highest and greatest good, which does include health and wellbeing, it is easy. There is no resistance once we have healed our relationship with food and ourselves. However, for a dysfunctional eater, making food choices for health reasons can often be disguised as diet mentality. It's more comfortable to choose the low fat options and claim it's for health when the reality is that choice is rooted in diet thinking. Your health will not be impacted by ordering a full fat latte as opposed to a skinny one. So explore the motivation behind why you want to order a certain thing. By getting into the habit of asking yourself a few questions you really can start breaking this habitual thought cycle. Here are a few to get you started.

Where does my desire to eat that food come from? Does it come from my diet thinking beliefs around food? Does it come from my desire to nourish my body? Does it come from my desire to feel good in my body? Does it come from my emotional association of not ordering that food? For example, does ordering a side salad instead of french fries make you feel less guilty than if you had ordered the french fries? That's emotional attachment.

So now it's your turn. This is part of the journey which can provoke anxiety and fear but I'm asking you to trust the process.

EXERCISE: BE A RULE BREAKER

....

Write down all of the food rules which you have chosen to believe around food choices. All of the rules which have come from dieting. All of the rules which you have read about. All of the rules which you may have created yourself. Be honest. Write them all down in what ever order they fall onto the paper. You might find it helpful to think of the times you tell yourself you 'should' or 'shouldn't' do something, there is usually a rule behind that!

I shouldn't eat after 6pm
I shouldn't skip breakfast
I should eat fruit in the morning
I shouldn't mix protein and carbs

When you have your list in front of you, sit with it for a few moments. Reflect upon how you feel. What does it bring up for you? Are there more than you realised? Perhaps less than you thought? How many contradict each other? Can you see why this has become confusing and impossible for you?!

I then invite you to let that list go and all the rules written on it. You can choose to do this in whatever way feels empowering for you. You can burn it if you wish or maybe cut it into tiny pieces and throw it in the bin. Perhaps you want to create some kind of ending the diet rules ceremony. There is no right or wrong way just whatever feels good for you.

Breaking rules is something we have been taught is wrong (and I suspect you are a good girl - most good girls fight food and their bodies but we'll talk about that later), so this is rule breaking with INTENTION and PERMISSION and also EMPOWERMENT.

As you do this, try and release any judgement and simply observe through the lens of curiosity.

What happens?
How do you feel?
What do you notice?
What comes up for you?
How does the food taste?
Don't forget you are doing this will FULL PERMISSION.

From this moment on you are taking your power back by breaking those diet rules and letting them go, loosening the reins and the restriction around your food choice. And in doing so you are stepping into a place of becoming more in tune with your body, allowing your self trust around food to slowly reemerge and your food freedom to eventually return. And indeed it will.

Throwing Away The Scales

Have you ever felt your jeans get tighter leading up to your period or you have days and sometimes weeks throughout the month when you feel more conscious of your body feeling bloated, sluggish or heavier?

You have? Wonderful, you are normal!

Our weight fluctuates naturally from one week to the next, from one day to the next and from one moment to the next as it is not static, it changes all the time due to the nature of our body being alive. So taking a snapshot in time by jumping on the scales at 7am every morning after having a wee and stripping yourself naked, will show you nothing other than how your water levels have changed, your hormone levels have altered and perhaps whether your bowels may need emptying (too much info?!)

Yet we become so fixated and obsessed by these moments in time by giving them a meaning far greater than what they actually are.

Your weight today will be different to tomorrow.
Your weight today is likely different from this time yesterday.
Your weight in 2 weeks time will be different from 2 weeks ago because you are alive and your body is constantly evolving!

That's why trying to maintain a number through restriction and obsession is near enough impossible, not to mention it being damaging for our mental health.

So let me ask you how many times a day or per week do you weigh yourself? I recall from my own personal story that I went through moments of becoming completely dependant on the scales. I would weigh myself multiple times a day, hoping the number flashing on the display was what I was expecting. I weighed myself as soon as I got up, before I got dressed, after I'd been to the gym, before and after I ate my meals and before I went to bed. I became a slave to the scale and there's a chance that you are the same.

We often believe that weighing ourselves daily helps us stay in control and keep check on what we're eating. That's what I believed too. Except the opposite is true. By using the scales to keep you on the straight and narrow, you are actually giving your power away by choosing to believe that your self trust is non existent and you need an external object to keep you in check. It also does nothing for your control around food. How often has the number displayed on the screen been higher than you thought and it's sent you into a day of picking, snacking, emotional eating and possibly even binging?

After 14 years of obsessively weighing my body, what did I learn? Nothing other than how the number on the scales dictated my mood for the day and how much power it had over my life. The problem with needing to monitor our weight is that we are allowing an inanimate piece of metal or plastic not only dictate to us whether we are allowed to have a good or bad day ('yeah I've lost weight' or 'no I've put weight on') but we also inadvertently connect that to our self worth.

SCALES CANNOT DETERMINE YOUR SELF WORTH. THEY CANNOT HOLD THE POWER TO TELL YOU WHAT KIND OF A DAY YOU ARE ALLOWED TO HAVE BASED ON THE NUMBER THEY SHOW YOU

You are so much more than the number on a scale.

The only thing that scales can tell you is the size of your gravitational pull to the earth, a completely and utterly useless number. It means nothing. Just like BMI. The number doesn't show your kindness, your intellect, your uniqueness. It doesn't show how many people love you or how you impact the lives of others around you. It doesn't show what you've accomplished and what you've been through in your life. So take your power back.

This is how you're going to do that:

EXERCISE: STOP WEIGHING + MEASURING

....

I am challenging you to get rid of, let go of and throw away anything which is connected to your need to monitor, track, measure and weigh, whether that be food or your body!

So that means getting rid of...

the scales in the bathroom for all the reasons mentioned above

the pads of paper in the kitchen where you scribble down what you eat

scales where you weigh food to work out their calorific, point or Syn value

any other piece of tech such as myfitnesspal and apps on your phone for calorie monitoring

ALL. OF. THEM.

I know this is likely freaking you out but there's a HUGE and EMPOWERING reason you HAVE to do this. It's called trust and starting to rebuild your trust muscle. Reconnecting to body wisdom and learning to listen to and trust what you hear is compromised when you have all this measuring and tracking stuff in your life.

It's one or the other. You can't do both.

So either you want to stay a slave to diets, food and weight obsession OR you want to stop the obsession and find your freedom. The choice is yours

Side Note: I can hear you shouting 'but how can I feel more in control if I can't keep track of my weight?!?!'

What would knowing your weight bring you? It's scary throwing the scales away, I know, but it's setting that intention of breaking free from all of this whilst reclaiming your self trust. Monitoring your weight, even once in a while, destroys self trust and keeping track of your weight isn't strengthening your self control either. It's actually making you trust yourself less, moving you further away from body wisdom and creating the perfect conditions for binging and overeating. That's not really being in control, is it?

SATISFACTION + ENJOYMENT

History has been teaching women for centuries that we should not acknowledge or honour our desires. Some teachings talk about it being wrong to have desires for it's the work of the devil whilst patriarchy has been controlling and suppressing us for a very long time indeed, telling us we should be ashamed for wanting to experience pleasure and enjoyment in all areas of our lives.

So what has this got to do with food? Well quite simply, eating should be enjoyable. It should be pleasurable. It should also bring about a sense of satisfaction, yet for many women it doesn't. How much satisfaction and pleasure do you get from eating?

Perhaps you enjoy food during the first few minutes but then your attention turns to feeling guilty about what you are eating. Perhaps you think that food brings you pleasure and satisfaction, but the reality is that for years you have eaten so fast and hurried, you hardly taste the food whilst you are eating it. Or perhaps if you are really honest with yourself, the whole topic of food and eating creates far too much stress for pleasure and satisfaction to even co-exist within the same conversation. It's super important to point out here that reconnecting to body wisdom forms the foundation of recognising satisfaction as if you are ever in your head while you are eating, you will find it hard to feel satisfied.

That was me. I became so fed up of the emotionally draining cycle which I had got myself into, that eventually food became such a stressor that even eating became overwhelming. I no longer knew what to eat, how much to eat, when to stop or even what my body truly desired to eat anymore. I had completely tuned out of my body wisdom and lost connection with myself and my desires.

Later in the book we'll be exploring the symbolism of dysfunctional eating and why we use food to fill voids within our lives but for now, let me tell you that one of those reasons is our desire for pleasure. Pleasure naturally brings about a feeling of satisfaction and this is where eating plays a huge role.

WITHOUT SATISFACTION OUR MINDS CONTINUE TO SEEK OUT PLEASURE UNTIL WE FEEL SATISFIED.

I want to demonstrate this point using a very typical diet focused example. Let's imagine that you are on a diet and salad is on the menu for lunch. Being a diet friendly salad, your plate is piled high with leaves, chopped up vegetables and possibly some baked or grilled chicken breast. You hold off on the dressing, wanting to be 'good' or you see how far a teaspoon of fat free dressing goes (the thought of that goop makes me heave!) You get stuck in and eat that salad as you are hungry and it's lunch time. Afterwards you find yourself no longer feeling hungry as it was a fairly big portion and being diet friendly you could eat as much as you wanted, so may have even overeaten the salad if you think about it.

Yet do you feel satisfied? Was eating that salad a pleasurable and enjoyable experience for you? It may have fed your body as you aren't hungry but did it feed your soul? Did it tick the pleasure box?

I suspect the answer to those questions is no.

Now here's the point which I really want you to pay attention to. If at any time you have finished eating a meal and yet you do not feel satisfied as it was not a pleasurable and enjoyable experience, what tends to happen next? I will give you a clue. Our minds are programmed to be seeking out pleasure all the time. So if your lunch or dinner was not pleasurable and didn't create satisfaction within your body, your mind knows and is now programmed to seek out a new source of pleasure which will hopefully lead to satisfaction.

The easiest way to do this is by seeking out other delicious foods and we've all done it; going through the kitchen cupboards looking for a biscuit yet feeling like a crazed animal as you are trying to be good on this diet, but the thought of biscuits will not leave your head! Or maybe you have found yourself obsessing about chocolate, cake or biscuits all afternoon, yet trying to conjure up a huge amount of willpower in order to resist these overwhelming cravings which are getting stronger and stronger as each moment which passes. So you find yourself substituting your craving for something off your 'good list' and end up eating for the sake of eating.

HOW MANY CARROT STICKS DOES IT TAKE TO SUPPRESS A CRAVING FOR CHOCOLATE? ABOUT 7 AND A CHOCOLATE BISCUIT TOO!

I remember when I was in my first corporate job in Germany and I would always eat healthy food at the canteen every lunchtime. All my colleagues referred to me as being the healthy one. My tray was always piled high with leaves, vegetables and fruit and other perceived healthy food yet I was weight obsessed at the time and health was not a factor in my food choices, it was more about restricting calories in whatever way I could. Yet unbeknown to my work colleagues for almost the entire time which I worked there, several afternoons a week I'd sneak down to the kiosk and buy some form of chocolate or crisps or candy and stuff them in my face whilst locked in one of the toilet cubicles. Or I would call in to the shop or bakery on the way home and find myself having a mini binge before I'd even walked into my apartment. I always blamed myself for my lack of willpower, lack of discipline and stupidity yet I never realised that my food choice in the canteen was actually to blame and all I was doing was trying to seek out satisfaction and pleasure which my mind was programmed to do.

So keeping in mind the importance of satisfaction, going back to the salad example, let's imagine a different one. Still a bowl of leaves and chopped up vegetables yet this time you are no longer dieting as you have taken your power back. You are reconnected back to your body and you have listened to what she truly desires. As food labels and rules no longer exist in your life you have complete freedom of choice so the salad has a creamy Caesar dressing. It's sprinkled with lightly toasted garlic infused croutons and sitting gently on the top is a fried chicken breast which has been cooked in real butter, salt and pepper and sprinkled on the top are some fresh grated Parmesan shavings, tumbling throughout the leaves. Is your mouth watering yet? You eat this salad with full permission whilst listening and tuning into your body wisdom as much as you can. You taste every mouthful. You savour the flavour and your taste buds come to life as you explore the contrast in textures. You notice how enjoyable and pleasurable this experience is. It's a really tasty salad. Interestingly towards the end you recognise that you feel satisfied, perhaps not even finishing it all as you know you can have a salad like this whenever you desire. You haven't overeaten, you don't feel super full but instead you have this nice feeling of satisfaction and you have no desire to rummage through the kitchen cupboards trying to find a biscuit or five.

Which salad would you like to eat next time? It all starts with food choice and permission, Try it. You won't regret it.

Side Note:

"What if I can't feel satisfaction in anything I choose to eat?"

Over the years I have worked with woman who, despite understanding the importance of getting satisfaction from their food, have been adamant they don't ever feel satisfied no matter what they choose.

Satisfaction from eating comes down to three things:

1. Are you eating things which truly satisfy you?

Sometimes we eat things we think we 'should' and they don't actually satisfy so be super mindful of your choice. Are your food choices coming from you or is there still an element of diet mentality present?

2. Is your body craving nutrients?

If you have spent any amount of time restricting and especially under eating, your body will be craving nutrients when you start your journey towards food freedom. This may show itself as you wanting to keep eating and eating and feeling like the satisfaction signal doesn't kick in. It will do eventually, I promise. This is a time to keep reflecting on these steps of ditching the labels, diet rules and how to reconnect to your body.

3. What is the symbolism of your lack of satisfaction?

The final reason is to look at this symbolically which we will be doing later in the book. How you do food is how you do life. If satisfaction whilst eating is challenging, what areas of your life do you currently not feel satisfied in? What part or area of your life do you crave satisfaction but can't seem to find it? Your relationship with food is simply reflecting this back to you.

LEAVING SCARCITY MINDSET BEHIND

Changing your mindset from scarcity to abundance is part of the food freedom journey

How often do you clear your plate even though you know you aren't hungry anymore?

Were you ever told not to waste food as there were starving children in Africa?

Something I have observed in pretty much all of the women who come into my community who are struggling with finding peace with food is they are operating from a lack mentality or scarcity mindset.

A scarcity mindset is the belief that nothing should be wasted as there will never be enough — whether it's love, money, food or anything else — and as a result, thoughts and actions come from a place of lack. Lack mentality is almost always learnt behaviour, it's a learnt response to our stories and experiences we have had in our lives up until this point, truly believing there isn't enough, there might not be enough and also that we aren't enough.

Typical scarcity mindset around food shows itself in these ways:

You can't stop once you start
You overeat as it tastes so good
You take food with you if you go anywhere just incase you get hungry

You worry about getting hungry so eat in advance
You binge on foods which you usually don't allow yourself
to have
You eat food in preparation of the diet starting as you know
there won't be enough choice once you start the plan

Yet here is a truth I need you to know. We live in a world
which has infinite possibilities and an abundance of everything and we know some people choose to see their glass
half full, whilst many see their glass half empty. Whatever
we focus on grows and wherever our attention is directed,
we get more of the same so what are you focusing on at the
moment?

Let's get one thing clear which is that diets create scarcity
mindset. Every Monday when you've started a diet, there
have been rules disallowing certain foods, telling you to only
eat at certain times and preventing you from eating based on
free will. As you are given this unattainable ideal standard and
expected to achieve it, simultaneously you are being told that
we are not enough and that we can't have more of what we
want. This leads us to overeat (just incase), keep on eating
when no longer hungry (just incase) and stuffing ourselves to
the point of feeling terrible (just incase the food runs out and
there might never be enough.)

One of the more common scarcity beliefs I see in dysfunctional eaters is 'I can't waste food so I'll eat it instead.' This
one is categorically rooted in lack mentality and probably
originates from the stories your parents told you or rather
their stories which they passed on to you. Here's a reframe,
whether you eat the food on your plate even when you know
your body isn't hungry for it, or you put it in the bin.....either
way it's still waste. Stop treating your body like a rubbish bin.
Waste is waste. If it is no longer required, it is surplus and it
is waste. Get rid of it.

Side Note: Most of our scarcity mindset is self created and something which we choose to believe based on stories, what we've been told or what we hear. However, I have had several clients who had personal experience of genuine poverty as a child, so their life experience had taught them that scarcity and lack was very real. They literally didn't have enough food to eat and despite their parents doing their best sometimes they went to bed hungry. As a mum myself that breaks my heart to even imagine the distress for everyone concerned, yet these early memories and deep rooted emotions stayed with these ladies for decades, understandably so, and it's not surprising that overeating and binge eating were the ways these early experiences manifested in later life for they still had that underlying fear, that scarcity mindset, that they might go hungry as they did in the past. If this is you then it's worth working with someone to help you change your beliefs around this and heal whatever needs to be healed.

EXERCISE: LEAVE FOOD

....

I want to challenge you to deliberately, intentionally and with full permission leave food on your plate. There is always more than enough. It will never run out.

If you feel fearful, anxious or sense resistance about doing so, here are some questions to explore:

What am I afraid will happen if I go through with this?
What am I afraid it will mean about me if I leave food on my plate?
Do the above fears have to be true for me? (Hint: answer is 'no!')
What would I like to choose to believe instead?

THROUGH THE LENS OF CURIOUS

Fighting food and your body is exhausting. It drains you, stresses you and takes up far too much valuable time when you could actually be living your life. We all have beliefs when it comes to food and our bodies, yet if we never question or explore our beliefs, how will we ever know whether they are true? How will we ever know what they are really representative of? How will we ever know if they are even relevant for us today based on when they first started?

Next time you find yourself overeating, binging, feeling guilty, ashamed and stuffed.......stop and start to explore everything by taking off your glasses of judgement. We cannot invoke change through judgement, it's never going to happen as it keeps us stuck in a self perpetuating cycle which seems never ending. Whenever we allow ourselves to move away from judgement and step into curiosity, it changes everything as instead of blaming ourself for having overeaten, we slowly start to find compassion, understanding and an appreciation for who we are, often showing us that we are doing the very best we can do in any given moment, which is true by the way. I get my clients to write in a notebook a conversation with themselves, simply through the lens of curiosity. No judgement. No expectation. No attachment. Almost like becoming an explorer in their inner world. I'd like to invite you to try it too.

Here are some questions to start you off:

- What's going on right now?

- How do I feel?

- Where do I feel it?

- How do I know it's there?

- What colour is it?

- What shape is it?

- What does it represent?

- Does it remind me of anything?

- If it wasn't about the food, what would it be about?

Even if you think you are guessing, it doesn't matter but carry on questioning through curiosity. Whenever you find yourself thinking you know why you are doing something, but you never seem to be able to change what you are doing, stop and question. There is often something going on a bit deeper than you have noticed so explore it.

Your Self Trust Muscle

The only way to get your self-trust back is to start working on all the underlying reasons you believe you can't trust yourself. Taking your power back with food is one of them!

If you trusted yourself fully with food and your body, you wouldn't be reading this book. Self trust is everything and it goes way beyond simply knowing what to eat for dinner tonight. If you struggle with trusting yourself around food, then you'll also more than likely struggle with trusting yourself with life choices and decisions in general, frequently asking for second opinions and second guessing yourself.

Now it could be that you've got this far and are thinking, 'how the hell am I going to know what to do without a diet or program to follow as I don't trust myself?' I hear this all the time, women doubting their intuitive feminine genius of knowing what to do with food, choices, decisions and life.

FREYA: STOP WEIGHING + MEASURING

....

When I started breaking away from dieting and getting rid of all the labels, it became apparent how little self trust I had. I wanted someone to tell me what to eat and what to do and I did feel a little lost for a while as I was so disconnected from myself and my body. The more I learnt to listen though, the easier it got and slowly but surely I noticed I was starting to trust myself more when it came to eating but also in the decisions I was making in life.

Chronic dieters don't trust themselves as they have forgotten how to listen. They have forgotten what 'she' (her body) sounds like and they have forgotten who they are underneath all those layers of body hatred, dieting, binging and restricting and beneath all the masks of who they are pretending to be. Diets have been teaching you for years that your body cannot be trusted, that your hungers are wrong and that your body is lying.

Everything which you think you can't do, is just a belief you hold and it's a belief which you are choosing to believe rather than the story which it is because the real truth is this:

You do know how to eat.
You do know what to eat.
You do know when to eat.
You do know when to stop.

Self trust is everything even beyond the realms of food and your body. It's about you trusting your beautiful, magical, powerful and wonderful self. Any woman who says she doesn't trust herself or says she has no intuition is really saying she doesn't allow herself to feel how she feels for it's not ok to be hungry for more and it's not ok to want what she wants.

EXERCISE: DEVELOPING YOUR TRUST MUSCLE

....

In what areas of your life do you not trust yourself?
What's stopping you from trusting yourself?
What beliefs do you have as to why you can't trust yourself?
If you could trust yourself, even just a little more today, where would you start?

STOP WAITING ON YOUR WEIGHT

Focusing on your body and your weight as being the barrier to your happiness isn't getting you anywhere

I asked Stephanie what she thought she'd do if she were slimmer. She said instantly she would feel confident to go swimming with her children and in that moment, as I saw her eyes fill with tears of sadness, I was truly heartbroken at her answer as I felt her pain being a mum myself. She had never ever been swimming with her children, even on holiday she had sat on the side of the pool or on the beach with a towel around herself, too embarrassed and ashamed to be seen, watching her children splash and laugh in the water with her husband, whilst she gazed from the sidelines as a spectator in her own life.

We worked together on helping her change her story. She didn't need to be slimmer to have fun with her children. They weren't judging her nor was anyone else. Only she was doing that, something you are probably guilty of too. Fast forward some time later and she's since started swimming regularly with her children and even wore a bikini on holiday last time they went away, something she could never have imagined doing a short while ago! She took charge of her own life and stopped allowing the stories in her mind and the beliefs from the diet industry to influence how she showed up as a mum to her boys, giving herself permission to create memories without needing a slimmer body to do so.

So many of my clients live each and every day living in the

past or the present with their weight unable to be truly present in their own life. I've lost count how many are waiting to shrink their way to happiness before they do the things they truly desire to do or they are desperate to have the body they had before children or when they were super sporty at high school, always thinking that someday they'll have the food and body thing sorted but until then they need to preoccupy themselves with it or things will get even more chaotic. This is when I need to remind them, and you, that we can choose to live that way and miss out on our lives or we can choose the radical act of learning to accept who we are now in a world which tells us that's not possible.

I know there is a part of you waiting for your weight to change before you do things. Before you embrace life. Before you challenge yourself. Before you go for your dreams. Before you allow yourself to be happy. Before you fully show up in life as the woman you are. You are literally waiting for your life to begin by waiting for your weight to change.

EXERCISE: PUT YOUR DESIRES ON PAPER

....

Without thinking too much about the answers, take a few minutes to write down all the things which you are waiting to do/be and have.

When I am slimmer I will.........

Now take a look at that list. How does it make you feel? Sad? Upset? Angry? Shocked? You have every right to feel however you feel.

Take a deep breath gorgeous as I'm inviting you with a gentle loving nudge to start doing those things on your list. Now. One at a time. Stop waiting on your weight, life is too short.

One final thing, can we talk about patience....?

Change can take a little time. It doesn't mean it will take for-ever, but it's going to take a little longer than a day or two and I know you are an impatient person, wanting everything yesterday. If you've read this far though, I also know that you are serious about ending this struggle and putting yourself back in your life where food is no longer in control, so I want to address something before we move on.

I know how real anxiety feels at the thought of stopping your diets. I know how real that panic is when you imagine al-lowing yourself to eat whatever you like, whenever you like it. I know how sad and upset you feel at leaving that vision of slimness behind which you have chased for years even though you know that you are too tired to chase it any more. I know how overwhelming the thoughts are about starting this journey towards food freedom as I was you a while ago. I get it but I also know how bloody amazing the other side is! The peace, the ease, the calmness, the stillness. Eating can be fun, easy, enjoyable and everything which it currently might not be for you. How you feel about your body can shift sig-nificantly with a bit of TLC and using the suggestions and resources in this book.

As you take these steps in the book into your day to day life, don't overwhelm yourself. Take one day at a time, in fact no, it's smaller than that. Take one bite at a time. Every time you eat without rules is a step in the right direction to becoming empowered around food. Every time you eat despite your diet gremlin appearing is a step in the right direction of you taking your power back. Every time you challenge your be-liefs around food and your body, is one step closer to find-ing your food freedom. Those bites will eventually turn into meals, which will turn into days, which will turn into weeks and then months and then years.

Finding your food freedom is learning to step into that place of discomfort which is holding you back and choosing to move forward regardless. Stepping into and acknowledging whatever comes up for you in the process and then taking responsibility for what you notice. Finding your food freedom is ultimately no longer hiding behind your eating or allowing 'it' to be who you have become.

One bite at a time gorgeous. You've got this.

STEP FIVE:
OVERCOME YOUR SELF
LIMITING BELIEFS

FOOD FOR THOUGHT

Food and how we feel about our bodies is just a manifestation of the bigger picture. It's a way of coping, dealing with, ignoring, burying, hiding from and sabotaging. It blocks us, stops us, prevents us and gives us a reason or rather an excuse of not doing, being, and creating what and who we truly crave to do, be or have.

I've said this before but being slim does not equal happiness. You might think it does right now as your entire world has been revolving around food, calories and weight loss, but when you slowly begin spending a little time unravelling all of the beliefs you have created around food and your weight, amazing things happen.

You find your food freedom.
You find your happiness.
You get your life back to truly enjoy every God damn moment of it in a body you are no longer desperate to change.

What surprises everyone who either works with me or gets into a conversation with me is the biggest part of helping someone break free from their self destructive cycle is mindset work around themselves. Once we get started after the initial conversations around food and eating, we rarely talk about it again, instead we focus on their minds, their beliefs and their stories. Mindset work really is the most important thing to give your attention to, not the food/weight/body stuff as it's never about those things in the first place.

We've spoken about diets and their contribution towards

your struggles with food, hopefully helping you understand the eating psychology behind some of your behaviours and I've shared with you some of the steps to actively take your power back by ditching the diets. After working as a clinical hypnotherapist for close to 10 years, I want to move on to a topic which truly fascinates me for two reasons. Firstly, because it was something which I had no awareness of whilst I was fighting food myself and I now know it was a huge missing piece of the puzzle at the time. Secondly, this is one of my passions, besides cake. I am obsessed about how our minds work and how our beliefs and stories not only influence our daily behaviour but how they also control much of it too.

Understanding your mindset and beliefs around food, eating and your body is so significant in your journey towards finding food freedom. No matter what you have tried so far, how long you have struggled with fighting food and yourself or whether you feel completely desperate to ever finding a solution, you can find your way out. In order for you to really understand why this topic is so powerful though, let's start by exploring how our minds actually work in the first place.

You've probably heard of the terms subconscious and conscious mind already but do you know what they are? Well your conscious mind is the part which you are using now whilst reading this. It's the part of your mind which analyses, comprehends and tries to understand what is going on whilst the subconscious mind is the part which you don't consciously use, you have no conscious control over it. If you think about how our heart beats, our body heals itself from injury and maintains our hormone levels all by itself without any conscious input from us, that is the work of the subconscious mind. The subconscious mind is also often referred to as the storeroom for in it you will find your stories, beliefs, emotions, memories & imagination along with any other things that you have stored in there from your past.

It's very similar to an iceberg in which the visible part sticking out of the water is our conscious mind with the majority of the iceberg being hidden under the water which represents the subconscious mind. Now here is where it gets fascinating. Scientists have shown and proven that most of our decisions, actions, emotions and behaviour depends on the 95% of brain activity that is beyond our conscious awareness, which means that 95% of our life comes from the programming in our subconscious mind. Our life reflects our subconscious programming and this comes down to the fact that the role of the subconscious is to create reality out of its programs and to prove those programs are true. If you have negative programming in your subconscious, 95% of the time you will recreate those negative experiences in your life. If you believe you are addicted to food, 95% of the time your behaviour will prove that belief to be true and you'll find yourself fighting food more often than not! If you believe you are a binge eater, 95% of the time you'll find yourself behaving how you perceive a binge eater to be by losing control around food. Once again, this proves your belief to be true and reinforces it all over again which is why positive thinking and willpower are futile as our subconscious mind is so powerful. That's why any time you have tried to avoid chocolate when feeling stressed as you know it's emotional eating, you have found yourself mindlessly standing in the kitchen devouring an entire bar and it's happened again. As soon as you forget to stay conscious, your subconscious is back in charge. It's that simple.

Our beliefs in particular, although a huge subject and one which I could write an entire book about, are worth spending a little time exploring. Whatever we believe to be true becomes true for us and shows itself as our reality. Imagine if you had a belief which was constantly being proven wrong, it would probably tip you over the edge at some point as you would end up internally fighting with yourself. Our beliefs create our reality, it isn't the other way around. If you believe you are a sugar addict or a food addict, your behaviour will match that belief giving you evidence which proves yourself right over time. If you believe you are a binge eater, the same thing happens. If you believe you can't stop this cycle of food and weight obsession, the same thing happens. So in order to fully find your freedom, as well as ditching the diets, you have to look at what beliefs are holding you back from being the woman you desire to be.

The thing is with beliefs is we don't go walking around everyday knowing what beliefs we have. We certainly don't go around questioning those beliefs either because for us they are the truth, much like a fish doesn't question whether it is in water, so a good way of identifying your beliefs about yourself is to finish off this statement:

I AM.......

I personally believe these two words are the most powerful in our language for whatever you put after them will not only become your reality as they are the beliefs you are carrying about yourself but they also become your identity. Typical ones I have seen over the years are:

I am a food addict
I am a binge eater
I am lazy
I am addicted to sugar
I am insecure about myself
I am not good enough
I am unloveable

Feeding your mind new beliefs as to who you are choosing to be is something which you cannot afford not to invest your time in, after all mindset work is about changing your thoughts and beliefs. It's about clearing out some of the things in your store room or subconscious mind so the voices in your head which criticise and judge you for having eaten that chocolate bar eventually become quiet. Mindset work is about rewiring yourself to feel body confident and to experience the joy of your incredible body without hating her or wishing she was smaller. Ultimately mindset work is learning to shift your focus and attention away from the things which don't serve you such as overthinking, overanalysing and trying to get things perfect and instead moving your focus towards things which do such as gratitude, happiness, fun, pleasure and feeling alive.

I hear women tell me they don't have time to work on their mindset every day and I just shrug my shoulders. The truth is you have to create the time to spend on this as every day you lose to your food obsession and body hatred is a day you could have fully lived and experienced life as it is meant to be.

So what beliefs are you going to start feeding your mind today about yourself?

EXERCISE: REWRITE YOUR BELIEFS

....

Your task now is to write out some new beliefs, through CHOICE. A belief is simply a thought you keep telling yourself over and over again, so if you have beliefs and labels which disempower you.....CHANGE THEM!

A quick example:

I AM calm and relaxed around food.
I AM fully connected to my body wisdom which gets stronger each and every day
I AM the creator of my own reality

I AM feeling more accepting of myself in every moment
I AM choosing to be kind and compassionate to myself
in as many ways as I can

Get the idea? Off you go! Have this list close to you and
get in to the habit of reading it, preferably out loud, several
times a day until they start to feel true for you.

YOUR UNDIGESTED STORY

A way to deal with indigestible feelings is by eating them

We are all spiritual beings having a human experience and part of being human is that life happens. We experience things which are challenging, things which are uncomfortable and sometimes things which are down right painful. All of these become part of our story which makes us who we are today. However, sometimes we can have stories which we have not fully digested. Experiences which still feel as real today as they did when they happened. Memories of incidents and events which still create an emotional charge should we bring them to mind and it's these undigested stories which not only feed our dysfunction with food but also with our bodies and with ourselves. We refer to these memories and experiences as trauma which can vary significantly in their severity but trauma affects us all on a deep soul level, the effects of which can last a lifetime, especially when we keep reliving it and re-feeling what happened.

Your thoughts, emotions, perceptions and experiences travel through your body and just like food they can be undigested, sometimes for years. If you take something in, mentally or emotionally, without releasing whatever part of that process contains the waste, the part you don't need anymore, then you will continue to carry that around in your body energetically and emotionally for a long time until you are able to release it. In the meantime food can become your best friend.

I remember speaking to a client a few years ago and she was irritated that I kept asking her to acknowledge and feel how she felt about something she'd mentioned several times.

I've spent decades avoiding ever going there and you want me to go there now on purpose?!?

Her response was exactly the reason why she needed to go there and she knew it.

From experience, I often see women holding onto events from their past which have now formed part of their identity and they believe it to be true, particularly around self worth.

Self worth is the degree to which a person values and respects themselves and is proud of their accomplishments and who they are. We often observe that weight and food control becomes the only measure of self worth for some women which leads to the constant self destructive cycle of feeling like they are failing, recurring bouts of stress and anxiety and feelings of inadequacy.

Lack of self worth ultimately comes down to not feeling good enough.

EXERCISE: YOUR UNDIGESTED STORY

....

What incidents, events and stories are still undigested within you?

What incidents have made you feel not good enough?

What have been the most traumatic parts of your story so far?

What have been the worst?

What things do you still think about and wish never happened?

Write them all down and then use something like EFT to help release them so they can be fully digested and let go. You'll find help with this in the resources at the back of the book.

Side Note: I have worked with many women who have had abuse in their story and these experiences had created a lasting belief about themselves and their bodies with many feeling ashamed and disgusted about their bodies along with a sense of blaming their body for what happened and for letting them down. As I mentioned trauma can vary in its severity but if you know there are aspects of your undigested story which feel big, scary and overwhelming to deal with on your own, find someone to work through it with you. If it isn't myself, find a reputable therapist in your area who specialises in trauma work.

YOUR FEARFUL INNER CRITIC

We all get scared. It's part of life.

I'm not going to sugar coat this gorgeous. Whilst embarking on your own journey towards food freedom, you may experience waves of fear and panic. A restrictive feeling in your chest, like you can't breathe. A sick feeling in your stomach that stays with you no matter what you do or whirling thoughts in your head which make no sense but you allow them to take over for a little while. Ditching the diets is exciting and liberating but can also be terrifying at the same time. That's normal. Completely normal.

Fear used to control me. For years. I was scared of everything. Things going wrong. Things going right! I spent my days wondering 'what if' and adding different endings to the thought. I had so much fear about life in general and what other people thought about me, but most of my fear centred around food and my weight.

I was scared to eat cake incase I put on weight.
I was scared to buy cake incase I couldn't stop after one slice.
I was scared to think about cake just incase I ended up buying some and devouring the entire thing.

Fear dominated my thoughts, kept me stuck in diet prison and in a life which wasn't joyful.

Up until now you'll have noticed that fighting food and your body is a time consuming and exhausting activity, often amplified and worsened by the dialogue you have with your inner critic. She's that little voice in your head telling you all the things which really pull you down. She's the devil on your shoulder telling you how much of a failure you are and how you'll never succeed as you don't have what it takes. She's that black cloud hanging over your head and the terrible knot in your stomach as you believe everything she tells you. Yet surprisingly that voice in your head is not always your enemy.

Our inner critic is really our ego which feeds on our insecurities, fears and concerns. It's that thing which keeps us in our comfort zone, even though it's not always comfortable in our comfort zone. Our inner critic keeps us with what we know rather than moving forward. Which brings me nicely to this. Safety and protection.

A long time ago, our ancestors would have had a real need to have stayed with what they knew. New things would have been dangerous. Venturing further afield could have cost them their lives. Challenging their 'normality' could have ostracised them from their community leaving them at danger of being unable to fend for themselves. That is obviously no longer true for us now a days, however, that primeval part of our mind is still functioning as if it's sole job is to keep us safe.

For many of us, when we have a desire to change something about ourselves and our lives, that inner critic or our ego jumps in and within a blink of an eye, we start questioning whether we really can do it, whether we have what it takes and whether it will work whilst self doubt gets back in the driver's seat frequently accompanied by fear and anxiety as passengers. Yet this is what I've learnt about fear over the years. It never goes away. As we progress through life we will experience some aspect of fear and apprehension which is normal as it's our safety and protection mechanism kicking in trying to keep us safe from the unknown. So I'm inviting you to acknowledge it for being there and then explore it with curiosity. Be more accommodating of those thoughts coming from your fearful inner critic. One of the things which I use frequently when I recognise my inner critic is to use a pattern interrupter, my favourite being 'isn't that interesting what just happened?' It defuses the thought and takes the charge away so I can then choose a different thought instead. I still have moments of worry, anxiety and every once in a while fear but the difference for me now is none of it centres around food, my body or my weight. It's other life stuff of juggling being a mum, wife and business owner!

I use my fearful inner critic as a guide for showing me what I need to address and work on. I no longer push it down with food or try and distract myself from it by beating myself up in the gym. I sit with it and ask myself 'what's going on...?' What are you really fearful of right now? What's the worst that could happen? Is that *really* the worst that could happen?'

Fighting emotions, especially fear, usually backfires as even though it may appear that those emotions disappear after your fourth slice of cake, they haven't and they will come back. And when they do, you'll know about it.

EXERCISE: TALKING TO YOUR INNER CRITIC

....

I find it helpful to observe through the lens of curiosity, recognise where your inner critic ends and you begin and listen without attachment such as - 'isn't that interesting she is saying that? I wonder why?'

Next time she makes an appearance, the inner critic/gremlin/ego, here are some questions to ask:

What are you saying this for?

What are you fearful of?
What's the worst that could happen?
What are protecting me from?

Questions to ask yourself:
What am I afraid will happen here?
What am I afraid it will mean about me?
What story am I telling myself?
Do the above fears or worries have to be true for me?
(Hint: Answer is 'NO!')
What could be a different outcome? Play with outcomes/results that would feel better. Feel into the possibilities.

STEP SIX:
FEEDING YOUR
HUNGRY SOUL

WHAT ARE YOU REALLY HUNGRY FOR?

We buy into the belief that we need to lose weight in order to have what we really want, when often it's just easier to believe that than to go after what we truly desire in the first place!

Women come to me because they feel exhausted with their food and body struggles, desperately unhappy but can't find a way out. They question themselves, their relationships, their lives and often believe if only they could get to grips with food, everything would be so much better. Yet I know, hand on heart, that for 100% of those women, the problem is not an external one. They think it is but it isn't.

I know exactly what these women are craving as we all want the same.

All of us are seeking validation.
All of us are seeking acceptance from others and from ourselves.
All of us are seeing connection.
All of us are seeking approval.
All of us want to fit in and be loved.
Most importantly *all of us* want to be ourselves yet for some reason we can't as we don't know who we really are, we don't know how to be our true authentic self or we worry what other people will think if we stopped pretending and embraced our true self.

These cravings, these non psychical hungers I refer to as Hungry Soul Syndrome or HSS. Hungry Soul Syndrome is when we have a real craving and hunger for more and a desire to live a full up life but not knowing how or what that looks like.

One of the most common symptoms of HSS amongst women and the reason you are reading this book is fighting food and being obsessed about our weight. Emotional eating, binging, food obsession, food cravings, over eating, restriction and rules around food are all surface layer symptoms of a much deeper and more profound issue. Yes there is an element of diet culture and food rules interwoven in there, but ultimately it is all metaphorical. It's superficial in so many ways. That's why trying to only fix the food stuff will never result in transformation or freedom as you are attempting to fix a bullet wound with a plaster. It will never heal. Any kind of food struggles or dysfunctional relationships around food and eating, underpinned by a desire to slim down and lose weight, are being driven by a soul which is hungry for more.

My food struggles turned out to be very symptomatic, symbolic and metaphorical. I had a real deep hunger for more which left me starving for much of my adolescence and my 20s but I didn't know it. I knew the life I had wasn't satisfying me and I was hungry for so much more but at the same time I hadn't realised that was the issue. My full time and attention went on controlling food and trying to lose weight.

I've realised since working with the women I do that each and everyone of us silently crave things in life so I want to ask you, have you ever stopped to think what are you really hungry for?

THE WEIGHT YOU THINK YOU NEED TO LOSE ISN'T OFF YOUR BODY, IT'S THE HEAVINESS FROM YOUR HUNGRY SOUL

It's so easy for life to take over. We spend our time juggling jobs, families and homes, frequently putting other people's needs before our own. Our days can seem monotonously routine as we follow the clock and follow the schedule and sometimes we give so much of ourselves that we become empty, losing ourselves in the process of life. We don't know who we are anymore or what we want and that's when we start to believe we aren't good enough. Not slim enough. Not successful enough. Not trying hard enough. Not doing enough. Not this enough. Not that enough. I know that's what you're experiencing too. You see deep down inside you've disconnected from your soul fed woman and from your real hungers. Replacing your truth with routine, structure and following the rules of what you 'should' be doing based on other people's exceptions of who they want you to be, all the while ignoring this emptiness within you which you are desperately trying to fill with cake, chocolate and bottles of wine.

Feeling that something is missing when you can't quite put your finger on what that is, quite honestly is uncomfortable. I know it is. We've discussed this already in the book about feeding our feelings so instead of looking inwards to find the answer, you start to look outwards and blame your cellulite for making you feel rubbish. You blame your lack of self control as being at fault. You blame your wobbly bits for being the reason you feel so fed up, low and lost in life. You blame your recent weight gain for your lack of confidence and why socialising is off the table as you'd rather stay in and hide away. Yet the answer will never to be found outside of yourself nor will it be found in a diet program, the label on a smaller size of jeans or the number flashing on the bathroom scales.

Overeating, binging, feeling out of control around food and blaming your lack of will power are all symptoms of someone who is disconnected from themselves and their true soul hungers.

Women who are hungry for more.
Hungry for happiness
Hungry for fun
Hungry for passion
Hungry for pleasure
Hungry for companionship
Hungry for acceptance
Hungry for finding themselves

Losing weight will not solve that hunger. Ever.

Counting calories, weighing food and your body will not re-solve the belief that you are not enough and that happiness is a destination which you haven't yet got to. Restricting plea-sure by taking out your favourite foods from your diet will not make you happier. A slimmer body will not eradicate the dislike you have towards yourself and the emptiness you feel inside nor will it make you more of a worthy person to expe-rience all that life has to offer. Finding real freedom around food and your body starts with you ditching the diets once and for all and then digging deeper into your relationship with yourself in order to become acquainted with your soul fed woman.

I want to introduce the 4 shifts which allow you to begin feeding your own hungry soul. It's only when you start telling yourself the truth can you begin to find the light in this seem-ingly never ending battle.

THE SYMBOLIC SUBSTITUTE

To a hungry soul food is an obsession, to a satisfied soul food is just food

Your relationship with food is a direct reflection of your relationship with life. How you do food is how you do life and vice versa.

Let's put it this way, if you crave sugar and stuff chocolate down your throat at any given opportunity, you are likely craving 'sweetness' as perhaps the sweetness of life is missing for you. If you rush your food and are a super quick eater, you are likely a woman who rushes through life and hardly takes a moment to be still and enjoy it, living in her head and always thinking about tomorrow and her 'to do' lists. If you overeat in fear there's never enough, you are likely to believe that you are not enough. If you find it hard to enjoy your food as no matter what you choose it simply doesn't satisfy you, then you are likely to not feel satisfied with life generally. If you restrict food and are forever not allowing yourself to eat, then you are also stifling your soul from tasting life fully and experiencing life with pleasure and excitement, in effect holding yourself back from ever truly being who you are.

Food is often used as a replacement for something else. It's a replacement for intimacy, connection, friendship, love and self-care as even though you struggle with it, it never fights you back. Food is very neutral, it's always there for you and it's easy for it to become your trusted companion for when you need it to be. It's easily accessible, easy to get your hands on and it never judges or criticises you. You can see why it becomes the perfect thing to use to fill these voids within your hungry soul.

I remember working with a gorgeous lady called Cath. She had been struggling with dieting and food addiction for years and during one of our sessions I asked her what she was using food as a substitute for. She sat quietly for a while before replying 'everything'. She said it was comfort, support, safety, reward, a friend and a lover. Honouring that gave her permission to begin the journey towards healing her relationship with food as she acknowledged she wanted more in life.

CATH: FOOD BECAME EVERYTHING

....

Food soothed me in ways which I needed and I had always thought emotional eating was my problem. I'd tried for years to overcome it. I found in my darkest times when life was dull, boring, overwhelming or lonely, food was my friend. I took comfort in it. I turned to it to feel love, enjoyment, pleasure and all the other things which were missing but hadn't recognised or perhaps even wanted to acknowledge.

When we turn to food for other reasons than physical hunger, it is simply a substitute for something else. And it's not just food. We can compensate and substitute things using cigarettes, shopping or alcohol. Many women with a hungry soul can display binge behaviours in many areas and drinking isn't an exception. Binge social drinking is not uncommon, is it? It might not even be in a social situation, it could be at the weekend at home with your husband or partner and you get through a bottle (or two) of wine as 'it's the weekend.' There is absolutely nothing wrong with drinking alcohol, however, if you feel that you are doing this as a distraction or for escapism then this is your opportunity to step back and to start digging deeper.

What I really want you to appreciate is that dieting, restriction, deprivation and beating yourself up will never help you feel better about yourself as it will never change your current environmental or personal circumstances. Even in a slimmer body your boss will still be an asshole, your relationship will still be stale and passionless and your feud with your best friend still won't be over. So instead of focusing on fixing your weight and body, what if you could start honouring what your soul is craving and feed it what it is hungry for?

Often when women recognise these non-physical hungers within themselves, even though it might bring some relief to actually have an explanation why they can't stop eating chocolate or they binge until they feel sick, it also brings with it fear.

Fear of change.
Fear of the unknown.
Fear of what might happen if they act on this information
Fear of what might happen if they don't act on this information
Fear of whether they can really trust themselves.
And I can categorically tell you that fear is completely normal yet it is also something which, unless you face it eye to eye, acknowledge it for being there but push through it regardless, it will prevent you from being who you are truly meant to be.

Fear keeps us small. Fear keeps us safe. Fear keeps us where we are. Fear keeps us stuck in this cycle.

KARA: FACING THE FEAR

....

I had to face my fears and there were plenty. I realised my soul was hungry for connection, spontaneity, adventure, excitement and more fun, which meant having conversations with my husband, changing things in my business, altering some of the routines I had got into which no longer fed my soul but rather sucked it dry and finding ways of being ok with how I felt.

If you are fearful of what people might think of you or have fear of rejection or fear of change itself, recognise it for what it is, it's your mind trying to prevent you from changing, it's a safety mechanism but keep going regardless. If the fear is truly paralysing then tapping (EFT) is an incredible powerful tool to use of which you can access a free training in the bonuses of this book, head over to www.soulfedwoman.com/bookbonuses

EXERCISE: WHAT ARE YOU HUNGRY FOR?

....

What if you could step back from your own food struggles and see it as a symbolic substitute for other things?

What if you could recognise that your relationship with food and your body is actually trying to bring your attention to other areas or issues within your life, which no longer want to be ignored and stuffed down?

What if you could start being honest and truthful with yourself about your life as it currently is?

I want to ask you....what are you really hungry for?
Adventure? Change? Connection? Passion? Purpose?
Fun? Creativity?
Write it all out!

The answer or answers will lead you towards ending your struggles with food and yourself, as long as you take action on what your soul is telling you.

RADICAL TRUTH TELLING

Self destructive habits show up when we aren't living in our truth

How often do you find yourself biting your tongue and muttering something under your breath when you walk away? Do you find yourself keeping your mouth shut and holding your emotions back too? If you do then you aren't alone.

One of the fundamental ways in which any woman can truly find her freedom with food and herself is by learning authentic self expression by acknowledging what she feels, needs, senses, desires and craves and expressing that unapologetically with grace and truth. This isn't, however, what the majority of us do. I've noticed that most women with hungry souls are people pleasers who put other people's needs and requirements above and beyond their own. They become that woman who wears a fake smile when speaking to her boss when really she wants to tell him or her what she truly thinks. They become that woman who begrudgingly goes to the family gathering but would much rather be sat on the sofa with a good book and a glass of something in her hand than play happy families. They become that woman who says 'yes' to everything for fear of being judged and not being liked and then wonder why they are so bloody exhausted when they spread themselves too thinly. We can find ourselves speaking from other people's points of view and going along with conversations which we don't really agree with but we are too afraid to speak up due to our inner fear of people judging us, being criticised or the fear of confrontation. Not wanting to speak up and express our truth is once again about safety which seems to be a recurrent theme.

Radical truth telling is essentially establishing healthy boundaries so as to keep all the goodness in rather than keep things out. It's creating space for yourself in your own life rather than giving that space to every person, neighbour, colleague, family member and their dog! It is incredibly satisfying for a hungry soul to feed it some healthy clear boundaries for often we crave things for us, things which light us up and which we are hungry for on our terms and not the terms of everyone else.

Any kind of pain, discomfort or unhappiness can be signs of having lived in the shadows of your truth for too long. As we've previously discussed, it's so easy to turn to food to numb out of that current reality and pretend it isn't there, so instead of talking to your partner about something which has been bothering you for a while, you swallow it down for fear of confrontation which leaves you feeling even unhappier plus nothing changes. Instead of speaking up about something at work you keep your mouth shut for fear of looking silly or people judging you and then you wonder why later on that afternoon you are craving chocolate like your life depends on it.

THE MORE OUR TRUTH COMES OUT, THE LESS FOOD NEEDS TO GO IN

At the peak of my binging and weight obsession, I was in a job which bored me despite the amazing salary, benefits and city centre apartment which people twice my age would have given their right arm for, but I didn't feel satisfied or useful in that role, added to that I was in a relationship which had gone stale with underlying trust issues and a constant fear of what the future held for me. Did I speak up and say anything to anyone? Did I start being honest with myself about how I was really feeling or what I really wanted? Of course not, I stuffed it all down instead. Night after night. Week after week. Month after month. For years. I look back at that time now and I can completely appreciate why I suffered from anxiety, panic attacks, low self esteem and low self worth. I chose to ignore myself and my truth for such a long time and my body and soul knew it.

Stepping into and speaking your truth can be challenging as, if you are anything like I was and almost all of my clients, you handed your power away years ago, after all society teaches girls that they should be quiet and 'proper,' not too loud, not too noisy, not too opinionated and not too emotional. That British-stiff-upper-lip mentality has once more left grown women across the country and further afield operating from a place of habit and programming, staying quiet instead of speaking up so as to continue being the good girl they were bought up to be by putting a lid on how they really feel.

If you have trouble saying no to things or you are unnecessarily apologetic as you fear conflict and judgement and you try and be the good girl most of the time, I'm inviting you to find your voice again! Your current lack of self expression and your obsession with food and your body are so closely connected, yet you've probably never fully realised to what extend.

DON'T BE AFRAID OF LOSING PEOPLE BY SPEAKING UP, BE AFRAID OF LOSING YOURSELF BY PLEASING OTHERS

When you begin to speak your truth, you start to strip away the layers of conformity and doing the 'right' thing to reveal the real you. The authentic you. Your Soul Fed Woman. The process of uncovering a fuller sense of your authentic self often reveals who you think you are is actually obscuring the complete you and from that place your soul becomes truly fed so food is no longer used to stuff things down or numb out.

EXERCISE: SPEAKING YOUR TRUTH

....

In what areas of your life, if you were honest with yourself right now, have you not been speaking up?

Where have you not been expressing your truth?

What do you truly desire which you are afraid to express?

Is it work? Your career? Your business? What about within your family or relationships (professional, personal and intimate?)

Good Girls + Shy Rebels

Do you consider yourself to be a rebel? Probably not as most of us have been brought up to be a good girl as we've just mentioned. We've been taught to follow the rules, do the right thing, say the right thing and be a certain way but being too much of a good girl doesn't allow us to grow into independent and confident women who trust ourselves implicitly.

Good girls do what is expected of them by politely agreeing and obeying to the rules and very rarely speaking up for what they want. Good girls don't complain or misbehave, they tow the line and avoid conflict in fear of being rejected, perhaps from having been reprimanded in the past and now believing they aren't worthy of having their own opinion or ideas. Perhaps they have felt intimidated at some point in their story for speaking up and now find conforming is easier than conflict.

I was a good girl for years and there is a very good chance that you are too.

Good girls often struggle with food as it's a way of rebelling by controlling one of the only things which they think they are in control of, subconsciously tired of doing everything the right way based on other people's and society's expectations and rules.

OLIVIA: I REBELLED

....

Growing up my mum was very demanding of myself. We had a fabulous childhood and I know that my parents loved myself and my siblings very much and still do immensely. Yet Mum in particular used to encourage all of us to do really well in school and to always be the best in whatever we did. There were many times when if I didn't get the highest marks or I didn't win in competitions, she'd question me as to why not. For a long time I always felt not quite enough for her so I used to like being the good girl, receiving the praise and recognition of doing the right thing and feeling like I was making her proud. It was only years later that I started feeling trapped and restricted by having to follow the rules and live up to the standards of what was expected of me that I started to rebel. It was never intentional but I know that's where my eating disorder came from. It was a way of having my own control and power over something which my parents couldn't do anything about.

In my years of working as a therapist, I can categorically say that rebellion against food almost always has its roots in rebelling against authority and authoritative figures. It's the good girl sticking her middle finger up and saying 'I'm not doing what you tell me anymore!' It doesn't have to be in the form of an eating disorder by the way, it's also every time you rebel against a diet or an eating plan, which as we know happens frequently. Your rebel makes an appearance to remind you to move away from being a good girl of following the rules and instead listen to your own inner wisdom.

I've worked with so many wonderful women who have spent far too much time being that good girl, they no longer know how to think for themselves, trust themselves or take steps towards creating their own happiness. When a woman has always been taught to listen to her parents or people in authority, to never question what she hears, to behave the right way and always say yes of what is being asked of her, she will never trust herself in the future, sentencing her to a lifetime of looking outside of herself for external validation that she is doing the right thing. Self esteem comes from the ability of knowing it's ok to rebel at times. It's ok to say no. It's ok to break the rules. It's ok to have desires and it's categorically more than ok to do things your way. An incomprehensible amount of women stay in bad relationships and jobs as they are fearful of leaving. Too many women defer to others to help make their decisions for them. Too many women go along with things which are not for their highest and greatest good or in alignment with their truth for they are too scared to listen to themselves. When we lack self esteem we find it challenging to choose the right path for ourselves as we lack self trust, so instead we ask other people for their opinion about what is right for us and some of us do this for decades.

Quite recently I did something I've wanted to do for years but I'd kept telling myself it wasn't what I'd do. Not me. What would people think? Here I am teaching this stuff and every once in a while, another layer of my own baggage comes up to be heard and healed, it's all a work in progress. As I step into an even more truthful and authentic version of myself, I allow things to fall away which no longer serve me and that story was one of them. I realised by not allowing myself to do something which I had a desire to do, I was conforming to being a good girl once more and I promised myself years ago that I would no longer play by the rules, instead I'd create my own and follow my soul. So I did and she led me to get a unique, designed by me, gorgeous tattoo on my lower arm and I bloody love it! It represents so much more than can be seen. It represents power, freedom and choice and will be a constant lifetime reminder that it's ok to be me. Now I'm not saying you need to go out and get your arm tattooed and your nose pierced (unless you really want to!) but I am inviting you to embrace your shy inner rebel for she will lead you to the freedom of being your true self. From that place you will not fight food or your body any longer.

EXERCISE: MEET YOUR REBEL

....

Where in your life are you being a good girl?

How do you feel about that?

What areas of your life would you love to be more of a rebel?

What's stopping you?

How can you embrace your shy rebel more?

What have you always wanted to do which you've been too afraid of doing as 'that's not what someone like me does?'

DO IT!

Less Doing And More Being

The present moment is the only moment available to us, and it is the door to all moments - Thich Nhat Hanh

You cannot feed your hungry soul what she is craving if you aren't embodied or connected to her. Being in your head won't help. We've already discussed reconnecting to your body through body wisdom which is crucial when overcoming your food struggles, yet it goes so much deeper than that. Feeding your hungry soul involves you learning to listen and pay attention, not just to your body and what she tells you about food and eating but equally about life in all of its deliciousness. If you realised the power you had within you, there would be no more second guessing or doubting yourself ever again. You would fully relax into and allow this incredible wisdom to guide you throughout life, in your decisions, your choices and anything you do. Yet I know that your default setting is to go into your head, in 'doing' mode, rather than in your body in 'being' mode. If you are in your head it is impossible to listen to your inner wisdom as your inner being or your soul is very much a body thing, so when you want to tune into your soul and let her point you in the direction of what she is craving or hungry for, you have to be connected to hear her, like tuning the radio signal in order to receive the correct frequency.

WE ARE HUMAN BEINGS, NOT HUMAN DOINGS!

You see when we fight food and our bodies we spend and

waste our lives worrying about the future and reflecting on the past, neither of which are real, they are simply figments of our imagination. Practicing the art of 'being' and living in the moment not only strengthens body wisdom but it also helps reduce overwhelm and eventually quietens down your inner critic which frequently references the past or the future.

For me being mindful, which is arguably what this is, means to be intentional. Choosing to be purposeful and deliberate with everything from our thoughts to our actions as when we are intentional we are fully in our power. I try and spend a few moments throughout the day to just 'be' where I reduce distractions and really go inside of myself a little bit more. I practice focusing my attention away from the external of what I'm doing or thinking in that moment towards the internal by going within myself and observing what I am aware of.

EXERCISE: SHIFT INTO BEING MODE

....

Start focusing and shifting your energy away from 'doing' all the time – the "to-do" list, doing this, doing that – and actually try and simply "be" a little bit more.

So how does that look? Well, maybe it could mean taking 5 minutes out of your day to simply sit, turn your PC off, get rid of your phone, find a place you won't be disturbed and actually start to tune into yourself. If your mind wanders and drifts that's perfectly normal but try and focus on something like your breathing or an object in the room.

These questions I always find helpful:

What am I aware of?
What am I noticing?
What feels uncomfortable?
What feels comfortable?

What do I need right now?

The more you listen to yourself, the more momentum and clarity you are going to gain in terms of what your hungry soul is craving and from that point you can truly overcome food issues and body insecurities.

STEP SEVEN: LIVING A FULL UP LIFE THROUGH SOUL NOURISHMENT

Vitamin P Deficiency

Ok I realise there isn't actually such a vitamin, however, in this case we are talking about 'P' as in pleasure. Are you pleasure deficient? A deficiency in Vitamin P leaves the individual feeling low, joyless, fed up with life and a sense of running on empty.

Humans are genetically programmed to seek pleasure and avoid pain. It's how our minds are wired. A lion chasing a gazelle is seeking pleasure, while the unfortunate victim is doing its best to avoid pain. Indeed, we can imagine any behaviour can be seen as either of these, or a combination of both and this is particularly true in light of our eating. We eat as we are seeking pleasure, something which we are programmed to do whilst avoiding the discomfort or pain of being hungry or feeling uncomfortable.

We can take this a step further though. Remember earlier in the book when we were talking about the diet salad without dressing and it was not pleasurable to eat so the chances are you'd end up searching for something else afterwards as you wouldn't have felt satisfied? The same is true in life. When you have a life which is enjoyable and pleasurable, you have no need to seek out that metaphorical pleasure from food. You don't need the handfuls of biscuits on the sofa as you are bored, or the family sized bag of crisps as you're feeling fed up for even with the demands of juggling work, careers, families and other responsibilities, you feel well nourished, soul fed and satisfied with life.

EXERCISE: GIVE YOURSELF A VITAMIN 'P' SHOT

....

Where do you get your pleasure and fun from at the moment? If you struggle to answer that question or the only answer you can think of is food, then this is your opportunity to dive into your truth.

Find ways of sprinkling a little bit more pleasure into your world by asking yourself:

What brings me pleasure in life?
What lights me up?
What satisfies and nourishes my soul?
How can I experience more of that today?

Be creative with this! It could be taking the time to drink your favourite coffee without being disturbed every morning, finding time to go walking in nature at least once per week, setting some boundaries so you have time to yourself for 2 hours on a Thursday evening to meet friends, go to an art class or try something new. There is no right or wrong way, whatever feels good for you.

Turning On The Woo-Woo

Spiritual hunger cannot be obtained from the physical level.

I would never have called myself a spiritual person years ago. At the peak of my disordered eating I wasn't into spirituality. I was brought up Catholic and had a Catholic education going to church pretty much every Sunday as a family until I left home at 18 to go to university. I never went again after that, partly through rebellion I guess but also as I was unsure of what I believed to be true. Yet I wasn't spiritual, I wasn't religious, in fact I didn't know what I was. It was only during my own personal journey towards recovery that I began exploring the concept of spirituality and what that meant and looked like for me and this is what I discovered. Spirituality is not a religion. Spirituality has no denomination. It is not about meditating sitting cross-legged under a tree whilst burning incense and reading angel cards, but if that fills your soul then by all means go ahead and do it! The true meaning of spirituality is being connected, staying aware, becoming more in tune with who we are as an individual and to others, connecting to our soul, our intuition and learning to trust and love ourselves unconditionally. It's the universal magic which pulses through our veins.

It is simply about connection. Awareness. Curiosity. Questioning. Reflecting. Belonging. Awakening. Whether that be to a God, a higher source, the Divine, the universe, angels, spirits, our inner being or something else, but without connection we become detached and separated for all human beings crave connection and a sense of belonging, we want to be a part of something. We want to feel loved, cared for, nurtured and safe so when parts of that connection and that intimacy are missing, it's easy to turn to food as a way of giving us what we need. Yet spiritual hunger cannot be obtained from the physical level. If what you are truly craving is connection then chocolate really won't help. If what you are truly craving is a sense of belonging, then crisps really won't help. If what you are truly craving is a sense of purpose in your life, you won't find the answer at the bottom of a bottle of Pinot Grigio no matter how often you look.

Being stuck in our own story as to why we can't stop eating, why our bodies look the way they do, questioning what's wrong with us and what we think needs to be fixed, will lead us to becoming a helpless bystander in our own life. Some of us may even slide into victim mentality, playing the 'why me' card, 'it's not fair,' and 'I'll never break free from this.' I did this for several years, during that time nothing changed, the drama continued, the feelings of shame and guilt intensified and the cycle never broke. Yet here's the thing I want to make really clear. Until you make a deliberate, intentional and empowered decision to step away from the drama and become curious and willing to question all those things which you have never questioned before, you will never begin to assume responsibility. This is where spirituality is incredibly important.

What if your struggles with food are actually part of your spiritual awakening?

What if you binge, overeat, fight food and hate your body because it's bringing you to a place of finally understanding why you do it and who you are? You cannot heal your relationship with food and ultimately yourself without becoming more spiritually aware and connected. Connected to you. Connected to something. Connected to your truth. Connected to your desires. It's all part of the journey.

I honestly believe that all women who embark on overcoming their food struggles are actually starting their journey of spiritual awakening, that includes you. It's an opportunity for growth, to become the best version of yourself that you can be and from that place, you naturally show up in a different way in all areas of your life. A better partner. A better wife. A better mum. A better daughter. A better friend. A better boss. A better business owner. When you find peace, that inner battle field is no more as you find calmness which will change you for the better.

Spirituality is a massive topic as there are so many aspects and different areas we could talk about so for now I'm going to keep this super simple. Meditation and visualisation are a great place to star. When we quieten our minds, we begin to hear our inner being speaking to us and that is the start of connection.

About 10 years ago I was introduced to the world of visualisation and meditation and I was completely sceptical at the time, I had never tried it and if I'm honest I thought it was a load of rubbish. However, that was then and now I am a true convert to using meditation to deepen my connection to myself and help me show up in life as a better, happier and calmer person. Before you think this might not be for you as it's too spiritual and woo woo, that's not what it is. Meditation over the years has shifted in terms of people's perceptions of it. For me, meditation is simply about having some quiet time where I am able to 'be', able to observe what's going on and also connect to my higher self. I believe that when we start to connect to that higher self or inner being, massive breakthroughs can happen for we make the space for something within us that knows more than we do consciously to guide and support us.

So if you haven't tried it before or you don't believe you are into that kind of thing, I ask that you stay curious about it. The more frequently you get into these states of mediation, the more you are going to be able to listen to your hungry soul and your inner wisdom which is whispering to you all the time but if you are constantly busy, doing and rushing, you don't have the capacity to tune in, recognise, acknowledge or listen and without any of those things, you will find yourself on a monotonous hamster wheel living a life which no longer feels deliciously satisfying.

In the bonuses to accompany this book, I have recorded a few meditations for you to get you started *www.soulfedwoman. com/bookbonuses*

FIND YOUR SISTERHOOD

What does the word sisterhood mean to you?

It's always interesting to hear the variations from this single word. Some people love it for it gives them a sense of safety, belonging, acceptance, love and kindness. Yet some people don't like it at all, perhaps due to past experiences with girls at school or women later in life and feeling left out, pushed out or isolated.

I think for the majority we have a hard time with sisterhood. Sadly, society has taught us to see other women as a threat. We compare ourselves to each other and we see every woman is a competitor in some way. We've all done it. We see other women and find ourselves casting judgment without know-ing anything about them by going on the defensive, keeping our distance and assuming the worst.

'She's more attractive than me'
'She's got a better body than mine'
'She's more successful than I'll ever be'
'She's got far too much make up on'
'She's so confident, I wish I was like her'
'She's a better mum/wife/daughter than I am'
'What is she wearing?! That looks awful!'

Generations ago women stuck together and I mean really stuck together. The bond between our female ancestors was so important and so significant within their communities. Women came together in circle to celebrate, hold and sup-port each other not tear each other down.

I realised years ago how much body shaming and diet culture is actually spread and created by women which is so terribly sad when you think about it. How many of the mainstream magazines which body shame celebrities are written and edited by women? How many of the journalists who cover stories about someone having lost weight or gained weight are female? How many of the articles which we see online and in print which pull another woman down, have been proof read, edited and published by another woman? It's actually pretty twisted when you really stop and think.

THE VERY THING WHICH TAKES OUR PLEASURE AND CONNECTION AWAY AS WOMEN IN SOCIETY, IS FUELLED BY MANY WOMEN THEMSELVES

So what can we do about it?

Well making a stand for yourself is the first thing. Turning your back on the parts of society which pull you down and instead surrounding yourself with women who inspire, empower and support you. Also starting to recognise your magnificence! Just because another woman appears more beautiful, successful or slimmer, does not take away your own beauty, success or attractiveness.

When I started Soul Fed Woman, the global movement of empowering women to free themselves from food obsession, body hatred and dieting, I must admit, I debated about using the word sisterhood in our description for a little while as I had a funny personal connection to the word. I didn't hate it, yet I didn't love it either. I was kind of neutral.

Yet there were no other words I could use to describe the space which I was being guided to create. A space which was judgement and criticism free, which was safe to share, explore and witness whatever needed to be where we all had each other's backs and where we could each be our authentic self, take off the masks and simply be us.

I've done quite a bit of inner work around the term sisterhood since and now I adore it. It means so much to me as it epitomises belonging, support and community, something which I know you are craving too.

The journey of becoming a soul fed woman, which starts by acknowledging your soul hungers and then taking steps to feed them, cannot be done alone. We all need that extra bit of help at times, that extra bit of guidance and that extra bit of loving encouragement. That's what Soul Fed Woman is all about. A space where life changing shifts occur and where we each move courageously into the direction of our true authentic self, allowing all which no longer serves us to fall away whilst supporting, nurturing and encouraging each other to step up to who they are truly called to be. This is your invitation to find your circle of women who you know have your back instead of pulling you down. We're waiting for you at www.soulfedwoman.com

Permission Is Everything

We sometimes forget that giving ourselves permission grants us the freedom we are looking for in all areas. Permission also truly satisfies a soul which is hungry for more. So what better way as we come to the end of this book than for me to remind you that you always have permission.

You have permission to let this struggle go now.
You have permission to stop the fighting.
You have permission to find peace, joy and happiness.
You have permission to leave the past behind you and no longer bring it into your present or your future.
You have permission to ask for help and support. As much or as little as you need.
You have permission to admit you are struggling. It's not weakness it's a sign of strength and success.
You have permission to ask for guidance. Always.
You have permission to leave things behind which no longer serve, empower or support you with your onward journey in life.
You have permission to let friends go who no longer get you and your path. Even if you have to tell them straight. You still have permission to do that.
You have permission to stop trying to fit yourself into a box. You are who you are. Perfectly imperfect in every way.
You have permission to be spiritual and still like to drink, wear heels and bright red lipstick. You can be everything and create your own definitions.
You have permission to let go of all comments or criticism from anyone who has ever told you or implied that you aren't good enough. Especially if that person was you.

You have permission to trust yourself and your body. All that head chatter is just trying to confuse you. Listen. You will hear your truth.

You have permission to eat cake for breakfast if you desire without guilt or judgement.

You have permission to eat something else for breakfast if you desire without guilt or judgement. It's always your choice.

You have permission to feel confident in your body. Now. Not 10lbs from now.

You have permission to be in your body. To feel safe in your body. You may not have felt safe before but what if you are safe now?

You have permission to say no and mean no.

You also have permission to realise that saying no isn't wrong or makes you a bad person. It does make you clear with boundaries.

You have permission to remember that no is a complete sentence and needs no further explanation.

You have permission to put into place as many personal boundaries as you desire.

You have permission to stop seeking approval from anyone other than yourself. You approve you. Always.

You have permission to drop the need for perfect. Perfectionism will keep you stuck. Moving forward despite perfect keeps you moving.

You have permission to create the life of your dreams. There's only you who can get in the way of what you desire.

You have permission to stay up late partying or go to bed early with a cup of tea!

You have permission to stop over-giving if it feels rubbish. Depleting yourself is good for no-one, especially you.

You have permission to recognise yourself as the goddess that you truly are. A child of the universe whose gifts are needed in the world.

You have permission to stop the bitching self talk. That inner critic isn't the real you.

You have permission to love stuff which lights you up, even if others thing you are strange.

You also have permission to not care what they think.

You do have permission to stop caring about what people think of you. Pleasing everyone is not possible. Focus on pleasing yourself and your life will flourish.

You have permission to fill your life with weird and wonderful.

You have permission to have bad days. And good days. And bad days. And good days.

You have permission to stop thinking you are a terrible mum when your little ones are driving you crazy. It's not you. They are here to test and challenge you. You are doing great.

You have permission to know what an amazing person you are. Friend. Daughter. Mum. Wife. Partner. Sister. You.

You have permission to be you. To stop hiding. To stop pretending. To just be you.

You have permission to be too much.

You have permission to believe in anything you like. Angels and unicorns included.

You have permission to take time for yourself even when you are busy. In fact on busy days take twice as much time for yourself. Seriously. Do it. It will change your life.

You have permission to practice extreme self care and self acceptance. In whatever form feels good.

You have permission to nourish your soul and body every day.

You have permission to stop punishing yourself for what you haven't yet done or achieved. Life isn't a race. It's to be enjoyed.

You have permission to stop sometimes and just be. It's Ok to be.

You have permission to dream big. Never stop dreaming.

You have permission to ignore the opinions of anyone who says your dreams are too big.

You have permission to stop justifying what you want in life. If you want it then go and get it!

You have permission to be in a loving and harmonious relationship.

You have permission to be in an imperfect relationship.

You have permission to be single.

You have permission to decide what is right for you.

You have permission to say what's on your mind. To find your voice and speak your truth. Swallowing that down will lead to issues later on.

You have permission to change your mind and your opinion whenever you desire.

You have permission to be whatever body shape you are. No need to change your gorgeous self to fit into society's perception of 'perfect'

You have permission to embrace your beauty without spending a fortune on creams and potions.

You have permission to be yourself and be more of yourself .

You have permission to have feelings and emotions. Don't run from them. They are your internal compass guiding you towards things which are wanting your attention.

You have permission to want things to change.

You have permission to no longer be who you have always been.

You have permission to do and want things which your family don't.

You have permission to forgive the past.

You have permission to forgive yourself.

You have permission to smile at the small things.

You have permission to do the things which feel good to you.

You have permission to feed your soul.

You have permission to be you.

Always

CONCLUSION - YOUR INVITATION

Information without action won't lead to change. Implementation is key.

I hope you've enjoyed reading this book and see it as having been a good investment of your time. What I've laid out for you is the last 10 years worth of working with my clients, learning from the best mentors and teachers and continuously working on myself. I wish at the peak of my food dysfunction I had been handed a guide like this. I really want you to see this as being your opportunity to shortcut the trial and error which I went through to find my own freedom around food and freedom to be unapologetically myself.

No matter how amazing a book can be and how much information you can obtain from it, it will never be a substitute for personalised expertise so if you want to integrate this book and get the personalised guidance and support too, I invite you to consider applying to work with me in my mentorship program. You can do that by heading over to www.soulfed-woman.com/help Alternately take a look at The Food Freedom Masterclass if you'd prefer a group program, details of which can be found at www.foodfreedommasterclass.com

In the meantime we have a growing community of incredible women across the globe, all of which are taking their power back with food and reclaiming themselves. In a society which is constantly talking about dieting and losing weight, please make sure that you surround yourself with different conversations like we've had in this book, find groups of women who aren't interested in pulling themselves apart as they ate a slice of cake and who aren't interested in diet talk! You'll find those women over in our invitation only community on facebook, as you have the book you are invited too! You can join our community here: bit.ly/hungrysoulsupport Throughout the year, there are live workshops and events so be sure to find out where the next one will be and come along. You'll find all that information on the website www.soulfedwoman.com/events

I want to end the book with something one of our gorgeous souls in our community shared. I'll hand you over the Jennifer:

I feel like we all share many challenges in here but don't always give ourselves credit for the progress we are making. Also, I see people still wanting the quick diet and exercise fixes and questioning why Rachel's way is worth sticking at so I thought I'd share my story so far....

I've known Rachel online for a few years but I only thought to start reaching out for help in January this year. I took advantage of this free group, her free resources and offers of a one off 1:1. I engaged in the group and it became like a sponge for new info and even won one of Rachel's mini programmes which also really helped me. I'm telling you this bit above to show you that anyone can get started. The basics Rachel is teaching in here are things you can go away and implement.

Back in January I felt disgusted by my body, I was ready to throw myself into another diet/exercise spiral that I knew deep down would fail again because I wasn't addressing the emotions behind it all. So I decided to throw myself into Rachel's stuff instead as at my current rate of dieting and relapsing over the last 4 years I was averaging one stone gain every year so what can I really lose by trying? I might be happier, I might learn something, I might make some breakthroughs, I might learn to trust myself.

So it's August, 7 months since I committed to following Rachel and not following diets and this is what happened:

- Despite all my fears about throwing out the rules I did not put on extra weight. It did fluctuate as these things do but overall, no change.

- I threw away all labels about good and bad foods

- I stopped all diets including diet mentality about what foods I allowed myself to buy or not

- my binging is massively reduced and I now know what emotions set me off and am working on those things

- I am more aware of my body and what she wants and needs

- I went on holiday and sat by the pool for the first time not giving a shit what I looked like in my bikini. I genuinely loved my body despite changing nothing about her appearance

- I started doing the things I'd been putting off until I was thin: I bought new clothes, wore the things I liked, started saying yes to social things, smiling more, having more fun, taking more time for me, investing time and money in my self-care and taking steps forward in my business

But my biggest achievement? I did it all despite losing one of my best friends to suicide and falling into a deep depression. For the first time I didn't reach for food, I had learned how to nourish my body, I'd learned how to feel her grieving and just accept how horrible and sad and heart-broken I was without stuffing the emotions down. Rachel helped me through that hard time by teaching me how to connect with my body again. I have chronic fatigue syndrome and add grief and depression to that and you create the fuel for misusing food. But instead I listened, accepted and found ways to give me what I needed.

For any of you who are questioning whether Rachel's way works I want you to think about what "works" really means for you. This is not a quick fix, this is not a weight loss group disguised as self-love. This is pure self-love and acceptance. There are no weight loss guarantees here. But what do you ultimately want:

- to feel accepting of yourself?

- to feel comfortable and confident in your own skin?

- to feel in control of your own destiny?

I know you think that comes with a size or a weight but it doesn't. I was a size 8 and I was a broken shell of a person. I'm a size 18-20 now 15 stone and I'm the most content and confident I've been in many many many years thanks to Rachel.

Give this way a chance. Give it the same dedication that you would to a diet plan or exercise plan and just see what happens.

Jennifer Ishbel

www.jenniferishbel.com

It may not be a quick fix but quick fixes don't work. This is a journey which takes a little patience and practice but the rewards are unimaginable. One day at a time gorgeous soul.

I believe in you

Rachel x

BIBLIOGRAPHY

Children, Teens, Media, and Body Image. January 21, 2015.

https://www.commonsensemedia.org/research/children-teens-media-and-body-image

Rachel Moss. Two Thirds Of Brits Are On A Diet 'Most Of The Time', Study Shows. March 10, 2016.

https://www.huffingtonpost.co.uk/2016/03/10/majority-brits-are-on-a-diet-most-of-the-time_n_9426086.html

WW (Weight Watchers) Statistics, Facts & History, October 9, 2018

https://www.reviewchatter.com/statistics-facts-history/weight-watchers

Olivia Goldhill. A nation of weight watchers: Is our obsession with thin making us fat? August 1, 2014.

https://www.telegraph.co.uk/women/womens-health/11003614/A-nation-of-weight-watchers-Is-our-obsession-with-thin-making-us-fat.html

Tammy Dray. Facts & Statistics About Dieting.

https://www.livestrong.com/article/390541-facts-statistics-about-dieting/

WC Miller. How effective are traditional dietary and exercise interventions for weight loss? August 31, 1999.

https://www.ncbi.nlm.nih.gov/pubmed/10449014

N. John Bosomworth. The downside of weight loss. May 2012.

http://www.cfp.ca/content/58/5/517.long

AB Goldschmidt. Which dieters are at risk for the onset of binge eating? A prospective study of adolescents and young adults. July 2012.

https://www.ncbi.nlm.nih.gov/pubmed/?term=Which+Dieters+Are+at+Risk+for+the+Onset+of+Binge+Eating%3F+A+Prospective+Study+of+Adolescents+and+Young+Adults

A. Janet Tomiyama. Long-term Effects of Dieting: Is Weight Loss Related to Health? 2013

http://www.dishlab.org/pubs/2013%20Compass.pdf

Brittany Brolley. The average women's clothing size explained.

https://www.thelist.com/105630/truth-average-womens-clothing-size/?utm_campaign=clip

Julia Felsenthal. A Size 2 Is a Size 2 Is a Size 8. January 25, 2012.

http://www.slate.com/articles/arts/design/2012/01/clothing_sizes_getting_bigger_why_our_sizing_system_ makes_no_sense_.html

*Kinsey Grant. **Weight Watchers Trounces Earnings Expectations as New 'Freestyle' Plan Booms. February 28, 2018.***

https://www.thestreet.com/story/14503050/1/weight-watchers-earnings-ceo-interview.html

U.S. Weight Loss Market Worth $66 Billion. May 4, 2017

https://www.webwire.com/ViewPressRel.asp?aId=209054

Oskar T Brand. Stay Beautiful: Ugly Truth In Beauty Magazines. September 23, 2016

https://www.youtube.com/watch?v=zIIKTNPP5Ts

Nicholas T Bello. Dopamine and binge eating behaviours. April 24, 2010.

https://www.ncbi.nlm.nih.gov/pmc/articles/PMC2977997/

Sarah Marsh. Eating disorders: NHS reports surge in hospital admissions. February 12, 2018.

https://www.theguardian.com/society/2018/feb/12/eating-disorders-nhs-reports-surge-in-hospital-admissions

Jill Fisher, 'Household Do's and Don'ts', *The Irish Housewife*, 1960

Weight loss: Average dieter follows 55 fad diets during their lifetime. Feb 8, 2018.

https://www.express.co.uk/life-style/diets/916328/weight-loss-plans-tips-average-person-follows-diets

National Eating Disorders Association : https://www.
nationaleatingdisorders.org

BEAT, The UK's Eating Disorder Charity: https://
www.beateatingdisorders.org.uk

RESOURCES

National Eating Disorders Association :
https://www.nationaleatingdisorders.org

BEAT, The UK's Eating Disorder Charity:
https://www.beateatingdisorders.org.uk

Soul Fed Woman:
https://www.soulfedwoman.com

Book Bonuses:
https://www.soulfedwoman.com/bookbonuses

Events: https://www.soulfedwoman.com/events

Private Mentoring with Rachel:
https://www.soulfedwoman.com/help

The Food Freedom Masterclass:
https://www.foodfreedommasterclass.com

ABOUT THE AUTHOR

Rachel Foy is a British eating psychology mindset consultant, clinical hypnotherapist, speaker, podcast host and founder of the Soul Fed Woman, a global movement to empower women to free themselves from food obsession, body hatred and dieting. A former binge eater and diet addict, over the last 10 years she has helped women across the world transform their relationship with food and themselves through her private mentoring, group programs, workshops, public appearances and seminars. She has lived in France, Germany and Dubai and now works from her family home in Cheshire with her husband and their two children. You can find out more at www.soulfedwoman.com

CPSIA information can be obtained
at www.ICGtesting.com
Printed in the USA
LVHW050916080419
613326LV00017BA/784